PINE

Reaktion's Botanical series is the first of its kind, integrating horticultural and botanical writing with a broader account of the cultural and social impact of trees, plants and flowers.

Published
Oak Peter Young
Geranium Kasia Boddy
Pine Laura Mason
Lily Marcia Reiss

Forthcoming
Yew, Bamboo, Willow, Palm, Orchid
and others

PINE

Laura Mason

REAKTION BOOKS

Published by
REAKTION BOOKS LTD
33 Great Sutton Street
London EC1V 0DX, UK

www.reaktionbooks.co.uk

First published 2013

Printed and bound in China by C&C Offset Printing Co., Ltd

British Library Cataloguing in Publication Data
Mason, Laura, 1957–
Pine. – (Botanical)
1. Pine. 2. Pine – Utilization.
3. Pine tree in art.
4. Pine tree in literature.
I. Title II. Series
585.2-DC23

ISBN 978 1 78023 101 3

An extract from 'Dark Pine' by Robert Service, from *Songs for My Supper* (1953),
is quoted on p. 187 with permission from the Estate of Robert Service.

Contents

☙

Introduction

Pines are trees of wind and fire and light. Wind carries their pollen from one tree to another, disperses the seeds of many and fans the fires that are often their nemesis. Fire feeds on the resin-saturated wood of mature and dead pines, and fertilizes the ground for their seeds to germinate. For some species it is an essential part of their natural history, the heat opening their cones and releasing seeds; and in fire-cleared ground pine seedlings receive plenty of light. Fire and light run through the history of pines in human culture as well, together with a paradoxical association with water and seafaring, and ambiguity in the vocabulary surrounding them.

There are around 100 to 110 species of pine (genus *Pinus*, family Pinaceae), depending on the state of taxonomic thought and the authority consulted.[1] They are evergreen conifers, bearing seeds in woody cones and needle-like leaves in bundles. As a group, they are not fussy about soils. Individual species have their foibles, but the genus provides examples that grow in alkaline soils such as dolomitic limestone, on sand dunes, in serpentine soils poor in nutrients and high in toxic minerals, and in boggy areas.

Pine trees need seasons. As the genus is frequently associated with northern climates, these are usually stated in terms of warm

opposite: A sugar pine (*P. lambertiana*), which the tree's European discoverer David Douglas called his 'longed for pine' species, growing in Yosemite National Park.

7

Paul Cézanne, *Mont St Victoire, c.* 1887, oil on canvas. Pine trees recurred in the work of Paul Cézanne, who, in a letter to Emile Zola, reminded the author of the pine on the banks of the Arc, whose needles had protected them from the sun, and wished that it should be preserved from the woodchoppers.

and cold, of spring, summer, autumn and winter; but some species of pine belong to the tropics, where the important distinction is between wet and dry seasons.

In many people's minds, pines are associated with the unrelieved dark green of North American boreal forests or the taiga of Eurasia. They grow where many other plants find it difficult to flourish – in subarctic conditions, on high mountains, in semi-desert and on seashores – but are rarely the exclusive tree species in these places. They keep company with other conifers, birches and oaks, with shrubs such as juniper, heather and bilberry, or with the vegetation known as sagebrush or *chaparral* in North America, or Mediterranean *maquis* species, depending on the region. Some species grow in savannah-like grassland. In warm climates they tend to be mountain species, but some grow down to sea level. They are tough survivors, tolerant of unpromising environments, although competition from other trees will crowd them out in good soil. In such circumstances they retreat gradually to less hospitable territory, and subsist there until conditions are right for re-expansion. They may appear as pioneers on open ground – fire-cleared soil, abandoned fields, clearings created by the fall of large trees – but in their shade grow species nursed along in their shelter, species that in turn succeed them, stealing the light from any young pines.

The idea of a domesticated pine seems odd, but one does exist: umbrella pine, also called Italian stone pine (*Pinus pinea*), of the Mediterranean. But it is Linnaeus's *Pinus sylvestris*, meaning 'the pine of the woods', known in English as Scots pine and named in many other languages – *piño bravo, gemeine keifer, sosna lesnaya, pin sylvestre*[2] – that northern Europeans think of as the archetypal pine tree. A tree with a vast distribution, of high latitudes and cold winters, of glaciated mountains from the Atlantic coasts of Scotland and Norway to the Pacific shores of Russia, it gave little hint to early European explorers of the richness and variety of pine species they would find in North America, China and Southeast Asia.

The taxonomy of pine trees is complex, and they are of huge ecological and economic importance, leading to a vast and unmanageable literature on the subject.[3] They also have deep cultural and social significance. As native forest, they provide special habitats and a connection with the spiritual world; their tenacity is admired in the Far East, and their foliage, shapes and cones have intrigued artists throughout the ages. As plantations the trees are harvested for timber, to make fibres and card, and as garden trees they provide attractive forms and colour. The genus includes one of the oldest living life forms on the planet; perhaps most importantly, the products of pine trees were essential as preservatives and solvents in a pre-mineral oil world.

one

The Natural History of Pine Trees

Pines, genus *Pinus*, are native to the northern hemisphere – North America, Eurasia and down through China into Southeast Asia. The British have a limited view of them, unless they have had the cause or curiosity to observe many species. Scots pine is most familiar to them: a handsome tree with short, dark foliage, small cones and orange bark on its upper branches. They might gaze, perhaps disparagingly, across blocks of plantation conifers, unaware that they are looking at lodgepole pine (*P. contorta*), native to North America, pass shelter belts of *P. nigra*, commonly known as either Austrian or Corsican pine, or admire ornamental specimens of Japanese black pine (*P. thunbergii*) in gardens. None of these gives the faintest hint of the variability of which the genus is capable, or of its range or habitats. In addition there are many subspecies, variants, cultivars (forms deliberately selected by gardeners) and hybrids, naturally or artificially produced.

The clearest point that distinguishes pines from their close relatives such as spruce and fir in the family Pinaceae is the needles, or leaves, 'long and small like Threds; hard, durable, and constantly green; pointed or prickly [sharp] at their Tops; surrounded at the Bottom with a membraneous Sheath', as the French apothecary Pierre Pomet reported in the late seventeenth century.[1] These emerge from dwarf shoots, which in turn grow from the larger, easily visible, long, woody branches of the tree. Firs (genus *Abies*) and spruces (genus *Picea*) are most commonly confused with pines; these two genera both have single needles all over the growing branches. Those of firs leave

Gayo matsu
(Japanese white
pine, *P. parviflora*),
19th century, ink
drawing. Clearly
influenced by
European botanical
drawings, but lacking
some essential
detail, this shows
the needles (which
leave the branches in
bundles of five), the
rounded cone, and
winter buds at the
end of the branches.

circular scars when pulled off, differentiating them from spruces, which leave a small, curved peg at the base, making the twigs rough.

The papery sheath (actually another form of leaf) binds the leaves together in a fascicle; inside this the leaves fit tightly together at the base, where a cross-section shows them like wedges dividing a pie. The number of needles per bundle is important for initial identification: depending on the species they grow in twos, threes or fives, or up to eights in some Mexican pines – although there are atypical species: parry pinyon (*P. quadrifolia*) with four leaves in most bundles, and single-leaf pinyon (*P. monophylla*) with only one leaf per bundle but still with a fascicle sheath, and therefore a true pine. The fascicle sheath, too, is an important identifier; in some species it is shed and in others it remains on the tree.

The drooping needles of the Mexican weeping pine (*P. patula*).

All details are important to the botanist, but this is not a book about botany. One thing remarkable to the observer of a group of pine species – for instance, in a pinetum – is the variety in colour, texture and especially length that the needles display. Some, especially in species from cold or arid environments, such as Rocky Mountain bristlecone pine (*P. aristata*), or jack pine (*P. banksiana* of Canadian boreal forests), are only 2–3 cm long. Needles may leave the branch in short, dense, stubby masses (the aptly named foxtail pine, *P. balfouriana*), or grow in tufts at the ends of branches (Korean pine, *P. koraiensis*). Individual needles might twist (Bishop pine, *P. muricata*, from southwestern North America; Chinese red pine, *P. tabuliformis*) or grow long and filament-like, up to 25 cm in Mexican egg-cone pine (*P. oocarpa*, in Spanish *piño de colorado*), droop gracefully in bunches over the cones (chir pine, *P. roxburghii* of the Himalayas) or weep (Mexican weeping pine, *piño triste*, *P. patula*). Some bear a Christmas-card frosting of white resin flecks (the bristlecone pines), curve in a graceful arc (Japanese white pine, *P. parviflora*), or show other distinctive features such as a layer of white wax on the inner surface (Martinez pinyon, *P. maximartinezii*, in Spanish *maxipiñon*). Colour, in many pines, is deep forest green, but the range includes a handsome blue-green (sugar pine, *P. lambertiana*), dull grey-green (gray pine, *P. sabiniana*) and yellow-green (sand pine, *P. clausa*).

One species, Krempf's pine (*P. krempfii*) of the Vietnamese forests, has scimitar-like needles 3–7 cm long and about ½ cm wide. These puzzled botanists so much on its discovery that they were uncertain how to classify it and suggested it be given its own genus, or at least subgenus – *Ducampopinus*. It is now considered likely to be a true pine.[2]

Although pines are colloquially called evergreens, the needles are actually shed. This happens every two to three years in most species, but foxtail and bristlecone pines retain their needles for up to seventeen years. John Muir (1836–1914), writer and champion of the natural environment of the Yosemite Valley, said that the foxtail pine was given its name by 'the miners on account of its long bushy tassels. It is by far the most picturesque of all pines.'[3] The habit of retaining needles gives foxtail pine branches their characteristic tufted appearance.

The cone, the fruiting body, consists of scales arranged in a spiral around an axis. It was also described by Pomet, who said that it begins

> by a Button, which arrives to be a large scaly Apple, almost round, or pyramidal, of a reddish Colour: These Scales which form it are hard, woody, thicker commonly at the Point, or Top, than at the Bottom [that is, where they join the central stem]; hollow lengthwise with two Cavities, each of which contains a hard Shell, or oblong Nut, cover'd, or edg'd with a thin, light, reddish Rind.[4]

The term 'strobilus', plural 'strobili', derived from a word that means 'turning', was adopted as the overall botanical term for the immature cones containing the reproductive structures of pine trees (and other conifers). Each tree bears both male and female strobili in spring. The male strobili, also known as pollen cones, are sometimes called 'catkins' or 'flowers', although neither male nor female strobili are technically flowers.

Male pollen cones on an umbrella pine (*P. pinea*), releasing a cloud of pollen to the wind.

Pollen cones cluster around the bases of growing shoots and are relatively small, up to about 15 mm long. They are usually creamy-yellow or tan in colour, but some species bear red, purple or pink pollen cones. Pomet described these cones as being 'of several membraneous Foldings . . . fill'd with nothing but a light Dust'.[5] This is pollen, produced in enormous quantities. Two minute air-filled bladders support each individual grain. Pines rely on the wind to distribute pollen and it can be carried vast distances. Near forests, it can be very noticeable: the early nineteenth-century North American botanist Stephen Elliott (1771–1830) wrote of loblolly pine (*P. taeda*) that:

> This species, (as I believe of all the real pines) . . . bears aments of sterile flowers [that is, pollen cones] in clusters at the summit of the branches . . . the flowers, when mature, discharge so much pollen, that [the] surface of stagnant pools appears to be almost covered with this 'yellow dust' . . . In the streets of Charleston, after heavy storms, I have seen small ponds margined with the pollen which had been born by the winds across adjacent rivers.[6]

The female cones, Pomet's 'buttons', are technically known as megasporangiate strobili. Initially small, they grow singly on the branch tips or around the bases of terminal buds (the buds at the ends of branches that progress the growth of the tree in the subsequent growing season). Oval or egg-shaped and a couple of centimetres long, they stand upright into the wind. Their spiral structure is clearly visible, the scales recurving slightly, fresh and pliable, thin and delicately beaded with resin drops along their curved edges. The colours vary according to species and are often vivid – pink, deep red, magenta or purple.

Female cones contain two types of scale – ovuliferous ones, which bear the seeds, and bracts, modified leaves, supporting them. Cut a young cone in half lengthways and the ovules appear as pearl-like, rounded shapes clustered along the vertical axis. Wind-blown pollen drifts between the scales, where it is trapped by resin. A grain develops a pollen tube penetrating the ovule wall at a point where it faces the axis of the cone, and cells inside both the pollen grain and the ovules divide once. The scales close up, their edges sealed by resin, and the cells become dormant until the growing season of the following year, when the ovule develops two egg cells.[7] Likewise, two sperm cells develop in the pollen tube, and fertilization occurs. The seeds develop, two per scale, cupped in dark hollows, their embryonic root systems facing the axis.

Branch of Scots pine tree (*P. sylvestris*) showing new season's growth and immature female cone.

Cones take two to three years to mature, drooping from the branches as they grow. Immature cones may be a brilliant magenta-purple, bright viridian or pale whitish-green depending on the species; their surfaces are shiny and textured with a complex origami of oval or diamond-shaped scale edges. As they reach maturity, they become the more familiar tan or chestnut-brown colour. Their common name, 'cone', derives from Latin and describes their overall shape, pointed at the top, curved below, the angle of a quadrant. On the exterior overlapping scales spiral from base to apex. Pick off the woody scales one by one and the arrangement around the central axis becomes apparent.

All pine cones grow to the same general plan, but they show remarkable variation in size, form and texture. Two overall pine-cone forms catch the attention. One is elongated and narrow, with slightly flexible, leathery scales and an elegant, slim curve springing from the peduncle that attaches the whole to the branch (associated with a major subgenus known as *Strobus*). The other (more typical of

The huge, spiked cone of the gray pine (*P. sabiniana*), native to California.

subgenus *Pinus*) is more compact, egg- or oval-shaped, with hard and woody scales on a shorter, thicker stem. Differences are apparent in details of the scales. In the slender, flexible cones, the exposed part of each scale is long from top to bottom, a deep scallop terminating in a small bump. In the more compact, woody form, the long axis of the scales runs around the cone, the exposed edges forming a network of close-packed diamonds, each with a ridge running like a backbone from side to side. In the centre of each is a more or less pronounced bump, often bearing a spike or prickle. The name for this bump – on the terminal edge of the scale in one type of cone, dorsal in the other – is an 'umbo' (Latin for the central boss of a shield). In some species it forms a woody pyramid. The shape and size of a cone, the appearance of the umbo and the presence or absence of a prickle are all important for identifying different species.

On some cones the prickly umbo is so obvious that it is incorporated into the name. Bristlecone pine cones, both immature and mature, literally bristle. The Table Mountain pine of the eastern USA gained its Latin epithet, *pungens*, meaning 'piercing', partly because of its prickly leaves, but also because the cone bears sharp, upcurved spikes. Shortleaf pine (*P. echinata*) has immature female cones that bristle like hedgehogs or sea urchins, and *P. muricata*, the Latin name of bishop pine, recalls the spiky murex snail.

Pine cones range widely in size, from jack pine, whose tiny cones are only 2–3 cm long, to sugar pine of Oregon and the Californian Sierra Nevada, with cones up to 50 cm long. Weight, too, ranges from a few grams for the smallest cones up to that of the 'big cone' pine, Coulter pine (*P. coulteri*), whose dense, rounded, oval, massive woody cones weigh up to 2 kg; Torrey pines (*P. torreyana*) also have massive cones, and in both species the scales carry prominent sharp hooks.

Several pine species, such as knobcone pine (*P. attenuata*), have cones that are noticeably lopsided. Jack pine cones are 'remarkable for curving to one side, which gives them the appearance of small horns', said John Claudius Loudon in the 1840s.[8] The asymmetrical cones of Monterey pine (*P. radiata*) have scales markedly larger on one side than on the other, and their off-set stems make the cones lean at an oblique angle when fallen. Species vary, too, in terms of how the cones open. In some this is immediately on ripening, when their seeds shed to the wind, the cones falling to the ground afterwards; but others have cones that remain attached to the tree, disintegrating scale by scale. 'Serotinous' cones remain closed on their parent trees, their scales sealed by resin, until the heat of a forest fire melts this and they burst, shedding seed over the fire-cleared ground. The most extraordinary example of this occurs in knobcone pine, whose closed cones hang in clusters on the tree for years, while the wood of the trunk and branches slowly expands beneath and around them, gradually engulfing their forms. The woody, pointed and slightly curved cones resemble in shape nothing so much as the abdomen of a wasp, giving the trees a surreal appearance, as if groups of giant insects were clinging at intervals to their limbs. Other species rely on external agents, especially birds, to distribute their seeds; these include whitebark pine (*P. albicaulis*), whose cones do not open even in fires.

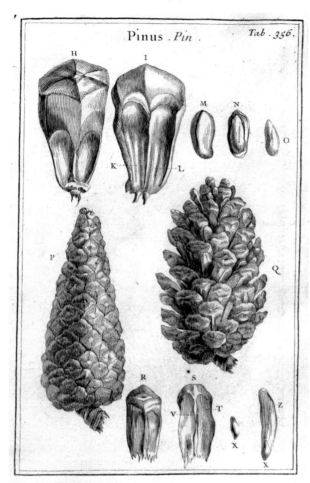

Anatomy of a pine cone showing the scales with the hollows which
hold the seeds in an illustration to Joseph Pitton de Tournefort's
Corollarium Institutionum rei herbariæ ... (1703).

These differences lead to variability in seeds. Inside a ripe, un-
opened cone the seeds lie in pairs, cupped in the hollows of the scales.
Each is enclosed in a thin, hard dark brown shell. Trees that rely on
wind dispersion have small seeds, each with a single, parchment-like
wing. Relative area of seed to wing varies according to the species;
one of the smallest, that of Japanese red pine (*P. densiflora*), is a tiny,
thickened point on a calligraphic sweep, a graceful exclamation mark

Clark's nutcracker in
an illustration by J. J.
Audubon for his *Birds
of America* (1840–44).

of a seed. The general shape and plan are repeated in varying size
and detail across species, but the seeds are never longer than about
3 cm in total. Some species have a detachable wing that grips the
seed coat from either side between pincer-like extensions. The wing
catches the wind as the seeds fall out of the cone and the seeds '"heli-
copter" to the ground, languidly rotating in still air, beating against
rocks and tree trunks in a stiff breeze, and possibly being dispersed
over miles'.[9]

Other pine seeds are large and appear wingless; the wing is actually present but reduced to the pincer-like arms. The trees they come
from are often called stone pines, a name that referred originally to
Italian stone pine (the reasons for the name are unknown, but
may relate to the hardness of the seeds). They include Siberian pine

(*P. sibirica*), dwarf Siberian pine (*P. pumila*), Korean pine (*P. koraiensis*), Swiss stone pine and various pinyon pines of the American southwest. Mexican pinyon (*P. cembroides*) was named after the arolla or Swiss stone pine (*P. cembra*), partly because of resemblances between the seeds. These pines have adopted a seed-distribution strategy that requires other organisms. Birds are the most important vectors, although other animals help – bears in North America and Siberia, squirrels and small rodents more generally.

The relationship between birds and pines has been most carefully studied in the mountains of Nevada, where whitebark pine has coevolved with Clark's nutcracker (*Nucifraga columbiana*) in a relationship that benefits both tree and bird.[10] These large grey birds remove ripe cones from the trees, clasp them between their feet and extract the seeds, storing up to about 90 in a special pouch under their tongues. Then they fly away and hide the seeds elsewhere, often several kilometres away. One study found that a flock of nutcrackers stored about a ton of seeds in one autumn. Inevitably, some are never retrieved and grow into trees.

Other bird species distribute pine seeds, notably pinyon jays (*Gymnorhinus cyanocephalus*), raucous birds that inhabit the pine woodlands of the American southwest. In late summer they prise green but ripe cones off the branches. They pick them apart, store the seeds in their throats and hide them for food in winter and the spring breeding season. The birds seem to discriminate between dark brown seed coats (likely to contain a good nut) and ones that are probably empty, which tend to have tan-coloured coats. Pinyon jays rely on pine nuts to feed nesting females and young, harvesting until all the seeds have either been collected or have fallen. Poor autumn crops seem to lead to a delay in breeding until new green cones appear on the trees the following summer. Researchers suggest that the visual trigger of the cones stimulates testis development in male pinyon jays.

Apparently, those brilliant emerald seed cones with their sparkling beads of resin are an aphrodisiac for the garrulous blue crow of the woodlands, persuading him that while late breeding may be poor breeding, it is better than no breeding at all.[11]

Inside their shells, pine nuts are small (even the largest, those of single-leaf pinyon, are only a little over a centimetre long), with an apparently insignificant aperture at one end – so small that one might assume that it had been caused by abrasion in shelled nuts. When the nut is divided carefully in half it can be seen that this is not so: it contains a minute, fragile, rod-like structure running from the hole through the length. At the rounded end, the rod has a tiny whorl of palest, delicate green, the whole being a pine tree in waiting, with a slender embryonic root and closely furled cotyledons.

Given the right circumstances, a pine seed on the ground surface finds sufficient warmth and moisture to enable the outer shell to split. The narrow end quickly develops a root, penetrating the soil. This helps to haul the other end upright, delivering water and nutrients to the growing plant and the cotyledons, which deepen in colour, expand and unfurl above ground. There are between five and 24 cotyledons, depending on the species. They are soon replaced by primary, then secondary leaves. This stage in the existence of some pines, especially longleaf pine (*P. palustris*), is known to botanists and foresters as the 'grass stage'. It lasts several years and is followed by a sudden growth spurt. Other species simply grow steadily. Young pines need light to grow well, and are crowded out by more shade-tolerant species.

Pine-root systems often develop in conjunction with mycorrhizal structures, fungi that colonize their outer surfaces with a pale coat. This, despite a sinister appearance, is a symbiotic relationship from which the fungi take nutrients, and which benefits the tree by facilitating the uptake of minerals, helping pines colonize poor soils.[12]

All sapling pines follow the same general growth pattern. A pseudowhorl (actually a very tight spiral) of secondary branches develops around the base of the leader. The tree expands rapidly over the space of a few years, the leader reaching ever upwards and secondary branches expanding sideways, giving the stereotypical pointed

Scots pine seedling
(*P. sylvestris*) emerging
from the seed coat.

conifer shape. It produces two different types of shoot. One type comprises the minute dwarf shoots that support leaf bundles; the other, much more obvious, the large, branching shoots that progress the growth of the tree. Pines grow in increments. Every year the growing tip divides to produce a leading shoot surrounded by a further spiral of branches. These new, initially upright stems – needles closely packed parallel to the direction of growth, with a pale, slightly waxy appearance – are known colloquially as candles. Growth is seasonal. In northern climates it takes place in spring, while in more tropical conditions it is dictated by wet and dry seasons. If planted in uniformly warm and humid tropical conditions, pines sometimes display a condition known as 'foxtailing', in which a tremendously long, ever-growing leader develops.[13]

The leader grows rapidly upwards for a few centimetres, then stops and forms a terminal winter bud. This contains a series of other structures – buds for pollen cones, and for dwarf shoots. Lateral buds sometimes contain shoots or seed cones, in which case they will not grow further. Once the shoots have expanded to their full length within a given season, the tree will not grow any more until the following year.

From the start, the seedling pine lays down harder tissues that strengthen its core. Initially these are composed of the starch polymer cellulose, but after about fourteen days more complex woody tissue, lignin, starts to form. It is produced in the spring growing period. Cells divide from the cambium, the layer of tissue one cell thick that covers the entire plant from the smallest root tip to the end of the newest growing shoot. On the inside they produce xylem, which carries water and nutrients from the root. Through the length of this run tracheids, elongated canals of former xylem cells, which conduct water upwards through the tree; these form about 90 per cent of the wood.[14] Their walls contain pits that communicate horizontally, allowing water movement across as well as vertically. Collectively they make up the sapwood, which is usually a pale creamy colour. As the tree grows, those in the centre gradually clog with minerals and acquire a deeper, often reddish colour, becoming heartwood. Physiologically inactive, this forms the strong core of the tree and is more resistant to decay than sapwood. New wood is produced early in the growing season, when hormones from bud growth stimulate the cambium to divide, producing new cells for both the inner bark and the xylem; early-season new-wood cells are wider and paler in colour than later, narrower, more lignified ones. Together the two form an annual ring.

In addition, pines have resin canals. Resin is not sap (which is a solution of nutrients in water). Resin is secreted by special cells, has a protective function and permeates all parts of the tree: needles, cones, branches, heartwood and the stumps of cut or dead trees. Resin is also visible on growing needles and immature female cones. The trunk is especially rich in resin, producing cells that surround vertical and horizontal canals running through it.[15] When a tree is damaged in some way – if a branch is broken, a hole is made by a wood-boring insect or a cut is made in the bark – the cells that line the resin canals become active. They may be remote from the site of the damage, but produce a flow of resin that ejects foreign matter and seals and protects the wound.

Resin is a factor in one of the most notable things about a pine forest: the smell. Although fragrant and unforgettable, this is difficult to describe, perhaps because it is more one-dimensional than perfumes associated with flowers. It is also more ephemeral. Nicholas Mirov, a botanist and chemist who spent his life studying pines, called it 'primeval' and explained that the essential oils of pine that emanate from the needles lack fixatives, the substances which give many perfumes stability. Pine resin 'consists of three kinds of substances: volatile oil, commonly called turpentine; the non-volatile part called rosin; and

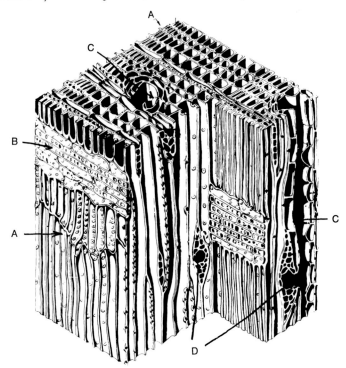

Diagram of the structure of pinewood. Vertical resin canals are shown at C, and horizontal ones at D.

George Inness, *Georgia Pines*, 1890, oil on wood. Pine trees in the warm climate of Georgia, U.S.: an image which conveys the claustrophobic quietness of some pine forests.

the high-boiling ingredients'.[16] The latter hold back the volatile oils, making them longer lasting. The volatile oil composition differs between species, giving each one a unique perfume. Compounds collectively known as terpenes are responsible for the smells. Some trees have simple mixtures of alpha and beta pinenes, which give the characteristic smell of turpentine, but many have unusual and distinctive chemistry. Lodgepole pines from the Rocky Mountains contain phellandrene, which smells like grass, and Italian stone pines contain limonene, also a component of citrus smells. Jeffrey pine (*P. jeffreyi*) resin contains no terpenes at all, but is composed of various aldehydes dissolved in heptane; it has a distinctive sweet smell described variously as resembling that of violets, vanilla or pineapple. Other species have their own distinctive but indescribable fragrances. This is one of the more inscrutable aspects of pines, and the reason for the existence of perfume in pine oil and resin remains unknown.

Outside the cambium the outer cells die and become compacted as bark, a protective layer against wounds and fires. As the tree increases in girth, the outer layers break up in rifts and polygons. In older trees the layers at lower levels can become several centimetres thick. Bark patterns vary from species to species. In younger trees the difference is not especially noticeable, although whether the bark is smooth or rough is an aid to identifying whether trees are placed by botanists in subgenus *Strobus* or *Pinus*. In older trees, patterns become quite distinct. The most striking and ornamental are seen in the Chinese species lacebark pine (*P. bungeana*), whose Chinese name means 'white bark pine', much esteemed in northern and central China. Lacebark pines shed bark in plates, giving irregular, grey-green and chalky-white patches that are very attractive. Cinnamon-coloured bark is a distinguishing feature of slash pine (*P. elliottii*); mature Scots pines have a distinctive glowing orange bark on their upper branches and Austrian pine (*P. nigra*) derives its Latin name, 'black', from the dark-coloured bark that contrasts with that of Scots pine. Whitebark pine has, as its name suggests, grey-white bark when young. Many species develop typical patterns: irregular, chequerboard like blocks (western white pine, *P. monticola*); plates (longleaf pine, whose orange-brown bark breaks up into small plates divided by deep, dark grey furrows); roughly rectangular, vertically oriented plates divided by deep dark furrows (ponderosa pine, *P. ponderosa*); or irregular, dark greyish-brown ridges separated by reddish-brown furrows (Monterey pine).

Eventually a tree achieves full height, as allowed by an interplay of genetics and environment. This is a subtle and highly variable element of the natural history of pines, which is partially responsible for the confusion that surrounded – and still to some extent surrounds – the classification of different species. Lodgepole pine is a notoriously variable species, partly because of the wide range of habitats it occupies. As a 'shore pine', it occurs as shrubby, twisted trees (as suggested by the Latin name) of relatively small stature, rarely reaching 30 m in height down the coast of the Pacific north-west of America. Inland, from the Yukon down through the Cascades and into the northwestern part of the USA, the trees grow tall and straight in stereotypical conifer spires of up to 50 m in height. Continuing inland, further south in the Cascade Mountains of Oregon and the Sierra Nevada, lodgepole pines (often known as tamarack or tamrack in this area) are generally trees of straight growth and slender trunk growing up to 40 m tall. The species was described by Mary Curry Tressider as

> often a most untidy tree; the dead branches clasping the lower portion of the trunk, the bark stripped and hanging, and the lower limbs drooping mournfully toward the ground combine to give it a most desolate appearance.[17]

The tallest pine species is sugar pine. 'No-one forgets their first meeting with a sugar pine,' said John Muir. On discovering it in 1826, botanist David Douglas wrote:

> and lest I should never see my friends to tell them verbally of this most beautiful and immensely large tree, I now state the dimensions of the largest one I could find that was blown down by the wind: Three feet from the ground, 57 feet 9 inches in circumference; 134 feet from the ground, 17 feet 5 inches; extreme length, 215 feet.[18]

Sugar pines have been heavily logged, and none of such broad dimensions survives, but botanists reckon the height to range from 40 to 60 m (130–97 ft) exceptionally up to 85 m (280 ft).

On reaching their full height, pines lose their conical shape and spread or broaden, their crowns becoming less dense, oval or rounded in shape, and their lower branches shedding to give less regular silhouettes. Pliny the Younger described the ash cloud from the eruption of Vesuvius in AD 79 as looking like a pine tree, 'for it rose high up into the sky on what one can describe as a very long trunk, and it then spread

opposite: Mottled colours on the bark of lacebark pine.

onto what looked like branches'.[19] He had in mind a multi-branched structure with a spreading crown, typical of mature pines, especially the Italian stone pine with its umbrella-like crown. In outline, the gray pine of the southwestern USA looks a little like an oak, but the foliage and cones distinguish it clearly from these. Sugar pines shed their lower limbs to give a tall, bare trunk, and have always captured the imagination of naturalists for grandeur and form:

> Completely disregarding the conventional spire-like forms of their associates, Sugar Pines toss out horizontally from the massive trunks a few, huge, irregularly-shaped, and length-ened branches.[20]

Chinese red pine takes its Latin epithet, *tabuliformis*, from the flat-topped shape the crown develops on maturity, and Japanese black pine develops a picturesque, irregular, windswept form. The twisted and irregular forms of pines and the notion of endurance and long-evity have an ancient connection in China, where the trees are a feature of many landscapes, notably precipitous mountain scenery. Much more recently, in Western culture, the age-contorted, pale, weathered spires with a few dark living branches of the aged bristlecone pines of the southwestern USA have became icons of endurance.

Few pines form shrubs, although the European mountain pine (*P. mugo*) of the Alps and Carpathians has a low, open, multi-branched form. Other pines, frequently stunted by the environment as well as genetics, are the partially dwarfed scrub Jersey, or Virginia pine (*P. virginiana*), which grows on poor soils on the eastern seaboard of the USA, and the dwarf Siberian pine, which grows in mat-like bushes and withstands the freezing winters of the Siberian tundra. Whitebark pines grow up to the timber-line in the Sierra Nevada of the south-western USA, where 'they are more like carpets than shrubs or trees . . . beaten down by the heavy blankets of snow and clipped smooth by the furious gales of winter'.[21] Sometimes the German word *krummholz* (*krumm*, bent, twisted, and *holz*, wood) is used to describe particularly bent mountain pines that have become stunted and deformed by exposure to tough environments.

Fire is a natural phenomenon in conifer forests, an integral part of the life cycle of pines. It is the death of many individual trees, but one that allows natural regeneration to flourish. The trees have adapted to it, achieving a dynamic equilibrium that allows them to dominate forests in which non-Pinus tree species would otherwise succeed them, crowding out the light from newly germinated pine seedlings. Low-intensity grass fires hug the ground, burning grasses and small shrubs, and doing relatively little damage to trees, but high-intensity fires, driven by wind, are hot and sweep through the crowns of mature trees, burning everything in their path and usually killing them. With their wood full of resin, pines are naturally flammable. They are drought tolerant and often grow in climates that have hot, dry periods of weather during which thunderstorms occur. Before humans learned how to make fire, the conflagrations in pine woods must have been due to natural phenomena such as lightning strikes. Man, accidentally or otherwise, must have vastly increased the occurrence of fire.

Evolution has given pines strategies against fire. The 'grass stage' in young longleaf pine is a defence against frequent low-intensity fires shortly after germination. The dense tuft of leaves protects the seedling for several years, while below ground a strong root system develops rapidly, acting as a food store if the topknot of leaves is burned off. Once the root is sufficiently developed, the tree grows quickly through the stage when it is vulnerable to a size large enough to resist low-intensity fires. Pitch pine (*P. rigida*) and Virginia pine exhibit a rarer strategy among pines: resprouting branches from burned trees. Red pine (*P. resinosa*) has a curious characteristic, probably related to fire resistance, in that roots of these trees in dense stands connect to those around them. If individual trees are cut, their stumps can remain alive, their root systems fed by those of the surviving trees.

A different strategy, used by trees with serotinous cones that are sealed until the heat of an intense crown fire warms them, is one in which the adult trees perish but young ones replace them.

The twisted, wind-polished wood of a dead bristlecone pine (*Balfourianae* spp.).

Although this is catastrophic for the individual trees, seeds are scattered onto ground newly cleared and fertilized by burning, ready to start the cycle again. Knobcone pine provides the most extreme example of this phenomenon. Bearing cones while still a sapling of a few years old, these and all subsequent cones remain on the tree until the heat of a fire opens them. Bishop pine, Monterey pine and lodgepole pine are also examples of these 'fire-dependent' species. Some pines – lodgepole pine, Monterey pine, jack pine – retain dead branches on their lower trunks that provide fuel for potential fires, making them especially vulnerable to high-intensity crown fires. Typically, the trees occur in single-aged stands, cohorts generated by fire.[22]

For animals and humans caught in fires, the story is one of fear and uncertainty. John McPhee, writing about the pine barrens (vast areas of poor soil that support little but pine and an understorey of grass and a few shrubs) of New Jersey, notes the 'V'-shape a typical forest fire describes on the ground as it progresses through a forest. The point of the 'V' represents the head fire, which leads lateral fires that spread out from each side. The line occupied by a fire may be 3 m or hundreds of metres wide, and the lateral fires may suddenly gain the fuel and energy to become head fires in their own right. Unpredictable in direction, intensity and width, forest fires are terrifying – the only safe place is on ground already burned.[23] Fire moves swiftly and threatens life and property; not surprisingly, the thought of a natural but unpredictable fire regime is unpopular with both foresters, for whom trees are a crop, and those who have chosen to make their homes in forests, for work or because they love the environment. The Canadian author and naturalist Chris Czajkowski gave a dramatic description of a forest fire that threatened her home on the remote Chilcotin Plateau of British Columbia:

Behind us a huge black wall of smoke had erupted. It had towered above us and the leading edge was beginning to curl

previous: The resins contained in living pine trees explode into fire, creating flames hundreds of metres in height.

A cluster of pointed cones on a knobcone pine (*P. attenuata*).

over the cabin . . . most alarming was the vivid orange colour
at the bottom of the smoke wall . . . the flames must either have
been huge or a good deal closer than we had been told. The
whole of the north ridge was haloed in orange. The water on
the lake . . . was a dull orange brown, the trees a sickly dull
green. White ash started to fall.[24]

Sometimes human communities learned to use fire to create a particular environment in pine woods. In eastern North America some
fires were 'managed' by indigenous American tribes who periodically
burned the undergrowth in the forests. They may have done this as
often as twice a year, burning grass and forest litter, creating a habitat
in which grasses for game animals such as deer and elk flourished, and
making an environment across which they could hunt more easily.
Regular, frequent fires reduced debris and burned at low intensities.
Manipulation of fire over a long time created open stands of mature
trees in some areas, such as the longleaf pine forests of North Carolina.
Early European settlers in North America followed native patterns
of fire management, but later arrivals had a view that did not accommo-
date such a dynamic natural environment, and fire became something
to be suppressed.[25]

In the absence of fire, pines tend to occupy sites on which other
tree species are unable to grow – poor, rocky soils in the Great Basin
of Colorado, serpentine soils on Cuba and in the Balkans, or sand
dunes in Les Landes in southwest France. Opportunists and survivors,
they flourish in a wide range of often unpromising circumstances:
'They . . . affect the cold, high and rocky grounds', wrote John Evelyn
(1620–1706) in his book *Sylva, or a Discourse of Forest Trees* (first published in 1664).[26] 'The debris of granitic rock may be considered as the
universal soil of the pine and fir tribe, and a dry subsoil an essential
condition for their prosperity', was the opinion of John Claudius
Loudon (1783–1843), although he admitted that 'they will grow on
all soils whatever, that are not surcharged with water.'[27] Although
in popular literature pine trees are associated with northern, cold,

gale-infested, rock-bound mountainsides, they grow happily in more fertile soils and gentle climates. Their problem is that faster-growing plants crowd them out.

The only naturally occurring southern-hemisphere pine trees are in a stand of Sumatran pine (*P. merkusii*) found in the Barisian Mountains of Sumatra, at two degrees south of the Equator, but a surprising number of species grow in warm northern-hemisphere climates. Sumatran pine and Caribbean pine (*P. caribaea*) – the latter grows on low-lying flats on islands such as the Bahamas and the Turks and Caicos – are both essentially tropical species, but several others rank as subtropical and grow in Southeast Asia, Central America and the Caribbean. In Cuba, Cuban red pine (*P. tropicalis*) grows in grasslands, or in stands in the Pinar del Rio province, the wet and dry seasons showing in the wood as paired light and dark rings. Hispaniolan pine (*P. occidentalis*) forms a forest in Haiti. Southeast Asian examples of subtropical pines include Vietnamese white pine (*P. dalatensis*) and Taiwan red pine (*P. taiwanensis*) from Taiwan and southern China. However, pines disdain humid tropical environments, in which they will grow, but not reproduce. Apart from such environments, and the most frozen of arctic wastes and arid of deserts, they have a wide distribution in the northern hemisphere.

The opportunist nature of pines is visible in open ground, whether it has been cleared naturally by forest fires or gales, or by man and then abandoned ('old field pine' is a common name for loblolly pine because of its invasive tendencies). Once seeded in such places they grow quickly – quicker than competing trees – and establish dominance. This can also be a weakness, for mature pines shade out their own light-loving seedlings. Eastern white pine (*P. strobus*) seeds on newly cleared ground, then outlives hardwood species that grow up with it; shade-tolerant species succeed them, and the white pines continue growing, towering over a forest in which their own seedlings can no longer germinate.

overleaf: Pine trunks, stripped by fire of needles and branches, look like stitches holding the fabric of a snowy Yellowstone landscape together.

The precipitous granite peaks of Huangshan, hung with pines, scenery admired and painted for centuries by the Chinese.

The pine tree as a survivor can be seen in high altitudes and high latitudes. Pines can tolerate cold and dryness on mountain ranges up to the treeline, or close to the Arctic Circle, where they grow as single-species forests, or in company with other conifers such as spruce or larch, or deciduous trees such as birch. The most extreme examples of survival are the Great Basin bristlecone pine (*P. longaeva*) and the closely related Rocky Mountain bristlecone pines and foxtail pines which live for thousands of years in the thin atmosphere and arid, rocky soils of high uplands in the southwestern USA. The oldest living single plant on earth is a pine tree, a Great Basin bristlecone pine known as Methuselah, whose precise location is known only to a few botanists and foresters. About 4,500 years old,[28] this tree was already venerable by the start of the Christian Era. In contrast, Monterey pines generally live for about a century.

The survival of a species is sometimes a matter of geography and luck. Monterey pine has an extremely limited natural range on a small area of the coast of California and three islands just offshore. This zone is bounded on the north and east by a climate that is too cold for the tree to survive in winter, and on the south by one that is too dry. It is an area prone to sea fog, which provides moisture, and 'It seems . . . reasonable to suggest that it is only a fortuitous accident of oceanography and coastal geomorphology giving rise to local sea fogs that have saved the species' that allowed Monterey pine to survive in this dry climate zone.[29]

Those who study pine trees recognize natural 'pine regions' in which pine flora is distinctive and specific in combination with particular trees and shrubs. Their boundaries depend on geology, topography and climate. North American pine regions run down either side of the continent. In eastern Canada and the USA they form a broad mass, spreading inland from the Atlantic coast across lowlands to the Great Lakes and the Mississippi plains, forests of great economic significance. The species gradually change depending on climate and soil, the most northerly being jack pine, graduating southwards through eastern white pine, red pine, pitch pine, Virginia pine, longleaf pine, loblolly pine, shortleaf pine and slash pine. Pine barrens are a feature of the poor soils of New Jersey, Virginia and North Carolina.

On the west coast, mountain ranges run north to south parallel to the ocean, providing habitats from sea level to about 3,500 m. Here a diversity of pine species grow in intricate mosaics, oriented roughly in north–south bands, the cold-tolerant species occurring at increasingly high altitudes as one proceeds further south, until they eventually meet conditions too warm or too arid. In the boreal forests of Canada, lodgepole pine holds sway. Further south the range of species increases to give some of the richest conifer flora in the world, including ponderosa pine and sugar pine; inland, the dry semi-deserts of Nevada and adjoining states are home to bristlecone and pinyon pines. These pine regions do not overlap, except in northern Canada, where lodgepole pine and jack pine occur together.

The east–west divide in regions relating to pine flora continues into Central America. The western one extends down the mountains of the Sierra Madre Occidental. The eastern one fringes the Gulf coast of the southern U.S. and Mexico, encompassing both the mountains of Central America and some Caribbean islands. These two southern pine regions overlap in a species-rich confusion in southern Mexico and Guatemala, where the Sierra Madre Occidental and the Sierra Madre Oriental converge.

Mildred Bryant Brooks, *The Pine Trees of Monterey*, 1935, etching.

Frederick E. Church, *Above the Clouds at Sunrise*, 1849, oil on canvas. A North American pine forest in a romantic, hyperreal representation, a world away from the activities of the loggers and lumber companies who were harvesting trees for the transatlantic timber trade.

Pine regions to the east of the Atlantic display a quite different pattern. In contrast to the richness and diversity of North American pine flora, Europe north of the Alps is a region of pine poverty in which the only native pine of importance is Scots pine. It has an enormous range, the largest of any pine species, from Scotland in the west to the Russian Pacific coast in the east. East of the Urals, two other pine species occupy huge areas – Siberian dwarf pine and Siberian stone pine. Korean pine overlaps the borders of several countries in the far east of Asia.

China and Southeast Asia are rich in pine species, but cultural and linguistic barriers make their study difficult for Western botanists. The complexities of Chinese geography, with a topography that includes broken mountain ranges, deserts and river plains, and climates ranging from cold continental to subtropical, also makes studying the distribution of pines in the region a difficult task. The country has about 22 pine species, some of which (such as lacebark pine) are both ornamental and relatively rare. The barriers that make the study of East Asia difficult are reinforced in Southeast Asia, where the details and distribution of subtropical species such as Khasi pine (*P. kesiya*) and Krempf's pine can be difficult to elucidate. Chinese and Southeast Asian pines are of great interest to specialists because the area is one in which new species are probably evolving. Japan has six common species, including Japanese black pine and Japanese red pine, both of which are valued as ornamental trees. The Himalayas, perhaps surprisingly in view of the association between mountains and pine trees, have few pine species, but these include the important chilgoza (*P. geradiana*), chir pine and Himalayan white pine (*P. wallichiana*).

The Mediterranean basin forms another pine region. Here, a long history of human interaction with the ecosystem in this area has obscured the natural ranges of pine species, but they are an important component of the vegetation and landscape.[30] About a dozen species are native, depending on how the region is defined, and exactly which trees are accepted as species. Canary Island pine (*P. canariensis*) is considered among these. Both Iberia and the eastern Mediterranean have been suggested as areas of origin for Italian stone pine, and the western Mediterranean for maritime pine (*P. pinaster*). One of the

Ivan Shishkin, *Morning in a Pine Forest*, 1889, oil on canvas.

Shi Tao, *View of Huangshan*, 1670, ink-painted album leaf. Pine trees are a feature of the work of the Buddhist monk and artist Shi Tao, who was deeply impressed by the scenery of Huangshan.

most widespread species of this region is Aleppo pine (*P. halepensis*), the only pine to occur widely in North Africa. It divides into two genetic groups – eastern and western – with debates about how the distributions of these relate to the past and present.[31] Other species, such as Austrian pine, are associated with mountains and have sometimes been subdivided so that, for instance, Corsican pine was in the past considered a separate species, *Pinus laricio*. The clearance and abandonment of land, fire and deliberate planting of pines for wood or pitch have all played their part in the complex history of pines in this region.

The distribution of pine trees over the northern hemisphere is the product of millions of years of evolution. The fossil record is fragmentary, but the *Pinaceae* originated in the Upper Jurassic (*c.* 150 million years ago).[32] Unambiguous pine fossils first appear in the early Cretaceous (*c.* 130 million years ago); the earliest, found in Belgium, is named *Pinus belgica*. On the other side of the world, Borneo, too, is rich in pine fossils. To state the changing distribution of pines with reference to present-day geography is futile because of the movements of landmasses over aeons of time. Some broad patterns can, however, be attributed to the distant past. A general division between pine species into ones with distinctly northern associations and those that belong to subtropical or tropical areas is probably due to the early Tertiary, a period of the Earth's history when the climate was significantly warmer and wetter than at present. During this time, pine trees appear to have retreated from latitudes that have a present-day temperate climate to (cooler) northern ones, or to upland areas in the tropics, spreading back when the climate cooled, but leaving an inheritance of division between warm-climate and temperate pines that exists to the present day.[33]

The absence of pine species across the Great Plains of North America is attributed to the existence of a shallow sea running north —south during the late Cretaceous, resulting in distinctly different pine flora to the east and west of this divide. In Eurasia, the north coast of another ancient sea, the Tethys Sea, which once stretched from the edge of an embryonic mountain range (now the Himalayas) to somewhere off the present-day coast of North Africa, allowed the spread of geographically well-separated but related populations – Canary Island pine and chir pine (native to northern India).[34] Ancient patterns of pine migration influenced by climate change during the Holocene ice ages are probably responsible for a pattern of pine distribution down the Malay peninsula onto Sumatra and into the Philippines, the trees moving southwards in the face of advancing glaciers as the climate cooled, and spreading back northwards once more as the climate warmed, colonizing new territory in the mountainous north of the island of Luzon.

The poverty of pine flora in northern Europe is also attributed to glaciation. Fossil evidence suggests that formerly a larger range of pine species was found in Europe north of the Alps, but glaciation pushed the trees southwards to meet a major barrier in the form of the Alps and mountains extending eastwards. Only Scots pine, a cold-tolerant species, survived this, probably in refugia (pockets of land with conditions locally clement enough for the trees to survive and reproduce).

Mary Anne Turner
after Adam Pijnacker,
Rocky Landscape,
c. 1835, print.

Once the ice retreated about 10,000 years ago, the pines spread northwards again.[35] Arid cold was probably the factor that also limited the number of pine species found in eastern Eurasia.

North America, with coastal plains and broken mountain ranges on the east side, and chains of high mountains running north–south on the west coast, provided much more scope for pine species to migrate north or south as the climate cooled and warmed again. The mountains on the west side of the continent were produced by tectonic activity that began 80 million years ago and still continues, providing varying habitats according to latitude and altitude. The fossil record of pine trees in Mexico is fragmentary, probably because this area was, and remains, seismically very active. It has also led to some of the most interesting and problematic aspects of the natural history of pine trees: Mexican pine species are highly variable, and botanists have always found them difficult to categorize.

European interaction with Mexico began with the conquistadors, following Columbus's discovery of North America. They found the

Scots pines (*P. sylvestris*) at Rothiemurchus, Scotland, today. The pine, birch and juniper woodland has regenerated to a point where it appears natural and little sign of the early 19th century logging which took place here survives.

countryside of 'New Spain' challenging: 'From Socochina we marched over a high mountain, through a pass, to Texutla', wrote Bernal Díaz in 1519, and

> arrived into a rugged and wild mountain district . . . the first
> night we had excessive cold . . . and the wind so keen, which
> blew across the snow mountains, that we shook again with the
> frost; indeed, no one can wonder at this, for we had come so

suddenly from the hot climate of Cuba, the town of Vera Cruz, and the neighbouring coast, into a cold country.[36]

As the Spanish discovered, steep mountains characterize southern Mexico – the product of geologically recent and continuing volcanicity. The Sierra Madre Oriental and Sierra Madre Occidental meet in a jumble of ridges and valleys and microclimates, with a rich genetic inheritance of pine species. The Spaniards were unaware of it, but they were moving through a region that would later be described, for its pine flora, as 'a natural forest genetics laboratory for foresters, botanists, taxonomers and geneticists . . . [a] quite remarkable and infinitely precious natural experiment'.[37]

The botanical world did not take much interest in Mexican pine flora until the mid-nineteenth century. 'In the year 1857 there was published in the City of Mexico a "Catalogue des Graines de Conifères Mexicains," by B. Roezl & Cie., in which were described eighty-two new species of Pinus', wrote George Russell Shaw (1848–1937), an American architect fascinated by the natural history of pines.[38] Benedikt Roezl (1824–1885) was a native of Czechoslovakia and the son of a gardener. He went to Mexico looking for novel species to send back to European horticulturalists, and described over 82 species of pine he considered hitherto unknown. Only one of these was an 'accidental hit', still accepted by botanists as Lawson's pine (*P. lawsoni*).[39] Roezl's catalogue confused thoughts about Mexican pines for decades. Enthusiastic and certainly unaware of a phenomenon elucidated by later botanists, Roezl

> unintentionally made . . . an extremely important discovery; in the Mexican highlands is located a secondary center of evolution and speciation in the genus Pinus: hence the never-ending and utterly confusing variability of Mexican – Central American pines.[40]

Shaw, in his *Pines of Mexico*, wrote:

Resin flows from an immature cone of Mexican white pine (*P. ayacahuite*).

A cursory examination of the specimens of Mexican Pines preserved in herbaria suggests a large number of species; the varied altitudes and climates of Mexico point to a like conclusion. Each excursion among the living trees, however, increased my suspicion that the numerous forms represent not many species but several varieties of new species.[41]

Much twentieth-century work on Mexican pines is inaccessible to the non-speaker of Spanish; a significant amount was carried out by Maximo Martinez (1888–1964) and Dr Jerzy Rzedowski (*b.* 1926), both of whom have trees named after them. The broken mountain ranges of Mexico and Guatemala give scope for rapid changes in altitude, rainfall and temperature: 'myriad microclimates' as Perry described them,[42] and the pine forests of these countries contain mixtures of several species growing in relatively close proximity. Due to the topography, climate and vegetation, 'Evolution in these pines is not something that only happened a million years ago, it happens every year.'[43] Left to hybridize and grow under natural circumstances, the pine trees of Mexico would no doubt continue to evolve with their environment, but the area is under pressure from population growth, and threatened by exploitation for firewood, construction wood and pine nuts, and by general environmental degradation. Genetic diversity in so useful a tree is a low priority for an impoverished and growing population.

two

Pine Trees in Myth and Reality

✧

'Pitys' was an ancient Greek name for the pine, and also a beautiful nymph. The simple version of her story merely says that Pan,
god of the forests, pursued her and in desperation to escape him
she changed herself into a pine tree. Another version of the story
relates how she was caught in a love triangle with Pan and Boreas, god
of the north wind, an angry character: 'Force is fitting for me. By
force . . . I overturn knotted oaks, harden the snow and strike the
earth with hail.'[1] Pitys preferred Pan, and in his anger Boreas threw
her against a cliff. Earth or Pan (stories vary) took pity on her and
turned her into a pine tree, her tears becoming the resin which pines
still weep from their wounds. Her myth tells poetic truths about pine
trees, of associations in the European mind with northernness, forests,
endurance and survival through mutability, and adds the detail of
the resin that pines and other conifers exude.

Other metamorphosis myths mention the Oreiades, mountain
nymphs who were born and died with their native pines, and the
maidens of Oikhaliai who, when the princess Dryope had departed
to join the nymphs, spread a rumour that she had been abducted.
The nymphs were angry and turned the maidens into pine trees.[2]

What other evidence is there of how Europeans thought about
pine trees in the distant past? The vocabulary of the Mediterranean
world included both *pitys*, which referred to pine trees generally as
well as the nymph, and *peuke*. This also referred to pines,[3] and gave
modern Greek the word for pine tree and also *Picea*, the genus to

Pan discovering Pitys being turned into a pine, from an Italian emblem book, 1550s.

which spruces belong. The Latin for pine tree was *pinus*, giving the generic name for the species. The sound/syllable *pi*, in *pitys* and pinus, traced back to an Indo-European base, is also found in *pix*, Latin for pitch, and the first element of Sanskrit *pitudāru*, as well as in pissasphalt, a now-archaic English word relating to bitumen (this definition from the *Oxford English Dictionary*). The *pi*-element evidently related both to particular trees and to a substance associated with them that was widely known since ancient times. 'Pitch', and similar words based on the same root, found its way into numerous medieval and modern European languages.

Latin *pinus* gave some southern European languages their word for pine tree: French *pin*, Italian *pignola* and Spanish *piño*. In Old English it was pin, the usage reinforced by the French spoken after the Norman Conquest. It was spelled variously – *pin, pyn* – before settling down to pine in the fifteenth or sixteenth century, and has remained in common use in English ever since. It was often applied to all evergreen conifers, including ones only distantly related to true pines, and was, confusingly, also used for some trees such as alder, which bear cones but are not conifers.[4] In the colonial period, English-speaking settlers in the southern hemisphere used 'pine' to name many exotic plants that displayed a generally conical, evergreen habit. Norfolk Island pine (*Araucaria heterophylla*), Chilean pine (or monkey puzzle tree, *Araucaria araucana*), Huon pine (*Lagarostrobos franklinii*) and celery pines (genus *Phyllocladus*) are just a few examples of plants with such names. Such colloquial use continues, and when a tree new to science was discovered in New South Wales in 1994, it became known as the Wollemi pine (*Wollemia nobilis*); but none of these trees belongs to genus *Pinus*.

Exploration and colonization by other nations also left linguistic marks – the French Canadians called a pine tree *un pin*, the Spanish in Mexico and the adjoining southwestern USA left the word *piño*, transmuted in American English to pinyon. A colonial legacy of

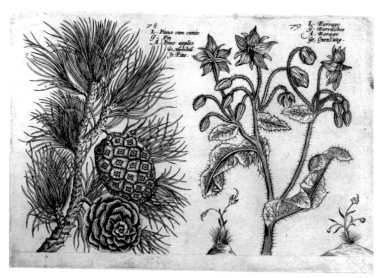

Print made by Crispjin de Passe the Elder after Jacques le Moyne, 'Pineapple', c. 1593–1603, engraving. Pine cones were known in various European languages as pine-apples; this branch bears both an open cone and a distinctly pineapple-like closed one, echoing the confusion of early explorers.

pin and *piño* also remains in southern-hemisphere names for non-pine conifers.

One spectacular case of misidentification was made in 1493, when Columbus's expedition was confronted with a fruit new to it on Guadeloupe. It was large, of a roughly conical shape and with a surface with a spiralling, scale-like pattern in hexagonal shapes, each with a papery spine in the centre. The only thing to which expedition members could relate it from their own knowledge was a pine cone; so they called it *piña*, brought it back to Europe and presented it to the king. Most European names, and the botanical one, *Ananas comosus*, are descended from the Brazilian Tupi Indian word, *nana* or *anana* (excellent fruit). The English, for once, agreed with the Spanish and called it a pineapple, their general name for pine cones at this period.[5]

In Britain 'pine' has a rival word, 'fir', derived from Germanic or Norse languages. As a collective name for conifers, 'fir' is sometimes used interchangeably with 'pine', especially when describing large numbers of trees viewed from a distance, or their timber. It still has strong currency. In botanical terms it is strictly applied as the English name for trees of the genus *Abies*, which is closely related to pines. It survives in some Scandinavian languages and as an element of a German word for pine, *keifer*. Russians, on the other hand, use the word *kedr*, derived from cedar, for some pine species, although *sosna* is the general Russian word.[6] Spruces take their common English name from an old word for the country of Prussia.

The peoples of pre-modern Europe clearly recognized pines and their relations, and evidently valued pitch, a product associated with them. Their knowledge, in the way a modern botanist would understand it, is less obvious. The Greek scholar Theophrastus (*c.* 371–287 BC) was one person who did leave a record, in *Enquiry into Plants*. Unfortunately for those unable to read the work in the original, Sir Arthur Hort, Theophrastus' translator, was not a botanist.[7] He used the word 'fir' even when he meant *pinus* species – 'fir of Ida' and 'fir of the seashore' (identified as Corsican pine and Aleppo pine respectively).[8] Pines cultivated for their edible seed – pine nuts – were also known.

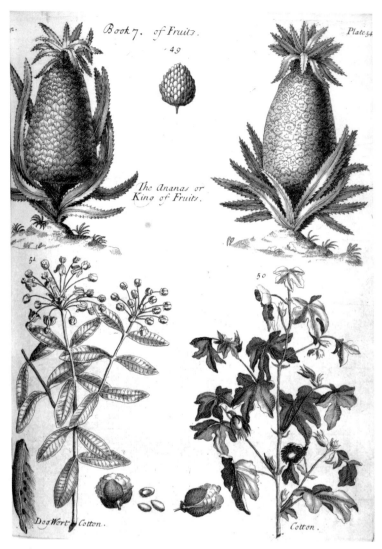

'The Ananas or King of Fruits', an illustration to Pierre Pomet's *A Compleat History of Druggs* (1737), a pineapple drawn to look like a pine cone.

Theophrastus consulted people with an interest in pines – torch cutters on Mount Ida, shipbuilders and resin tappers. His informants varied in their opinions about the natural history of pine trees, and he said that the Arcadians had decided views about them (even though pine trees were uncommon in Arcadia), and 'then dispute

David Kandel,
'Thannen und
Lerchenbeum',
illustration to
Hieronymus Bock,
*Kreuter Büch darin
Underschied* (1546).

altogether the nomenclature'.[9] Theophrastus was dealing with problems that have exasperated taxonomists to the present day. One is that 'It is by their use that different characters are recognised'[10] — that most people are interested in pine trees (as well as most other plants) for their utility. The other, unrealized until the late nineteenth century, is that even within species, pines can vary widely in form, depending on habitat. Observations were confused by the belief, current at the time, that trees were male and female.

Nicholas Mirov, who studied pine trees in the twentieth century, commented that the names given to pines and related conifers by European scholars of classical literature were often hopelessly confused, but considered that the Greeks made a distinction based on size and bearing, calling scrubby, resinous pines used mostly for pitch *pitys*, and tall, stately mountain pines *peuke*. Later, Russell Meiggs, a classicist who had also worked in the timber trade, concluded that the differences Theophrastus described between *pitys* and *peuke* were impossible to reconcile, and further confounded by varying usage of names in different areas. He considered that five pine species were significant: Scots pine in Macedonia and around the Black Sea; Aleppo pine; maritime pine, for resin, in Italy and the western Mediterranean; Austrian pine and *P. laricio* (formerly indicating Corsican pine, now considered Austrian pine); and Italian stone pine for pine nuts.[11]

Information about the natural history of pines from other classical authors is scant, their observations being mostly incidental or relating to practical uses. Pliny the Elder (AD 23–79) apparently recognized three pine species (translated by Mirov as Swiss stone pine, Scots pine and Italian stone pine) and recorded two words that have persisted in pine-related botanical vocabulary, *pinaster* and *taeda*. Pinaster was a wild pine that grew along the coast near Rome. *Taeda* was a more mysterious term. It literally means torch, and confused early modern botanists for years before the realization that it could apply to any old, diseased or dead conifer with the capacity to flare up if it caught fire.

The other area that provides much early evidence for human thought and interaction with pine trees is China. Here, pine trees (which transliterate from Chinese to English as *sung* or *song*) have occupied a special position in human consciousness for millennia. They appear to have had some of the associations anciently ascribed to oaks in Europe, especially resistance to the ravages of time,[12] and Shouxing, the Chinese god of immortality, is usually shown standing at the foot of a pine tree.

Pines are recorded as trees to be planted on the tumuli of Imperial tombs sometime during the late centuries BC, and the *Shan Hai Ching*, an ancient compilation of myth and geography about China, frequently observes that they grow at the tops of mountains. The literature includes many references to pines and their products; the Chinese accumulated an enormous practical knowledge of botany, including pine trees in general. Pine trees yielded soot particularly valued for ink; all parts of the tree were regarded as useful against pests, and there was evidently much knowledge relating to the planting

Fresco of a pine tree, c. 30 BC, from the Villa of Livia, Rome.

and cultivation of pines.[13] From about the twelfth century AD onwards, Chinese scholars observed and recorded that the number of needles per fascicle varied and could be categorized, well before Europeans had noted this and established it as an aid to identification, but the sources conflict over numbers of needle per bundle and are difficult to reconcile with species observable in modern China.

European botanical knowledge of pines apparently advanced very little for about 1,500 years from classical times until the early modern period. Most literature referred back to Theophrastus or was of a practical nature, concerned with subjects such as using pitch. The inhabitants of medieval Europe were intent on survival, and their philosophical thoughts were directed towards monotheistic religion rather than observations of the natural world for its own sake. They

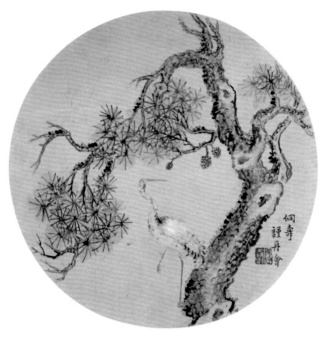

A pine tree and a crane in a Ching Dynasty Chinese painting by Tongshou. In Chinese culture, both tree and bird are auspicious and symbolize longevity.

must have continued to think in generalized terms of pines (or firs, according to their linguistic background). Identifying trees for pitch, wood and other products was their purpose, and any fine distinctions they made are no longer apparent.

The modern botanical idea of pine trees as a distinct group began to evolve around the end of the sixteenth century, with a more philosophical and careful reading of ancient texts. The Bauhin brothers, Jean (or Johann, 1541–1613) and Caspar (or Kaspar, 1560–1624), were physicians and scientists working in Geneva, sons of another Jean Bauhin who had been physician to the queen of Navarre. Jean Bauhin the younger, in his *Historia Plantarum Universalis Líber Nonus* (published posthumously in 1650), discussed the meanings of terms used by Theophrastus and complained of confusing terminology (as many concerned with pine trees continued to do). Caspar worked on botanical nomenclature, distinguishing between species and genus.[14]

Woodcut illustration to Olaus Magnus, *History of the Northern Peoples* (1555), showing trees of the northern countries including a pine or fir tree on the left.

Herbalists and apothecaries, who needed to identify plants correctly, also left descriptions. Pierre Pomet in the latter part of the seventeenth century wrote about four pine species – the one cultivated for pine nuts, and three wild pines, including a diminutive, shrubby one called the wild sea pine.[15]

The idea of the genus *Pinus* was formally introduced into botanical literature when Joseph Pitton de Tournefort (1656–1708) described seven genera – *Abies, Pinus, Larix, Thuja, Cupressus, Alnus* and *Betula*.[16] In *Species Plantarum*, Carl Linnaeus (1707–1778) limited the genus *Pinus* to ten species. As a representative he chose the wild pine of northern Europe, Scots pine, and gave it the Latin name *Pinus sylvestris*, pine of the woods. The others he named were Italian stone pine (*P. pinea*), arolla or Swiss stone pine of the Alps (*P. cembra*), and two north American pines, eastern white pine (*P. strobus*, using an ancient word meaning 'turning', related to strobilius, the ancient Greek and modern botanical name for the pine cone), and loblolly pine (*P. taeda*, using Pliny's word for torch). He also placed a cedar, a larch, two firs and a spruce in the genus. Given that several pine species were known to plant collectors by that time, it seems strange that Linnaeus did not describe more; it has been suggested that possibly he wanted to indicate a range of species in a field that was expanding.[17]

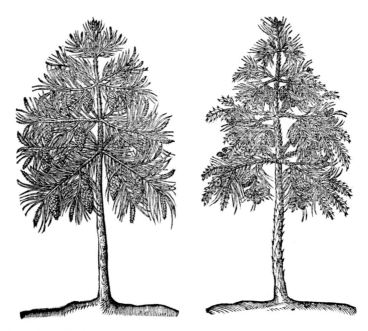

Ilustration to Rembert Dodoens's *Stirpium historiae pemptades sex* (1616), showing the pine of the woods and the pine of the seashore.

The genus *Pinus* may be 'a distinctly "natural" genus',[18] but it still needed elucidating, as Linnaeus' inclusion of firs, larch, spruce and cypress, and the continued use of common names showed. 'I discovered some pines which I am pretty confident are spruce-fir', wrote the naturalist James Robertson in his journal on 10 June 1771 en route from Braemar to Banffshire through the Scottish Highlands.[19] Circularity and tautology persisted in the names given to conifers; the early nineteenth-century botanist David Douglas referred to all conifers as pines, and spruce pine is still the common name for the North American species *Pinus glabra*.

Pines were confusing. 'The difficulty and obscurity of the GENUS PINUS have long been remarked and regretted by botanists', said Aylmer Bourke Lambert (1761–1842) in what must be the most beautiful book ever published on pine trees, *A Description of the Genus Pinus*.[20] Physically imposing and huge in size, with engraved plates by Ferdinand Bauer in the grand botanical tradition, it detailed all the pines (and other conifers) that the author had access to, either growing or as herbaria specimens. Lambert, a man of independent means, died in poverty as a result of following his obsessive interest in conifers. His fabulous book with its careful descriptions and glorious plates is, unfortunately, a bibliographer's nightmare, 'published in seven parts between 1803 and 1807 in a manner so irregular that copies vary in contents'.[21] A second volume followed in 1824. 'Difficulty' and 'obscurity' marked Lambert's publication, and unfortunately followed it as well. More species existed than Theophrastus or Linnaeus could have dreamed of, and they grew in a huge range of habitats. Before the late fifteenth-century voyages of exploration, Europeans had little opportunity to observe a wide range of pines. For people from northern Europe, they were simply the pine of the woods, Scots pine, and a very well-travelled inhabitant of the Mediterranean world might have had the opportunity to observe about twelve species.

By the late eighteenth century, all this had changed. North America, especially, was far richer in pine flora than anyone familiar with only *Pinus sylvestris* could imagine. Botanists accompanying exploratory voyages were followed by plant hunters charged with finding novel species that could be profitably raised for the European market. Their expeditions were often dangerous, as David Douglas's dramatic account of his discovery of the sugar pine illustrated. Douglas knew that a gigantic species of pine grew somewhere in the mountains of northern Oregon, having seen both the seeds and a cone. In October 1826 he made an uncomfortable journey into the hills, and with the help of native people located some of these trees, called in the local Umpqua language *natele*. As the massive trees were too tall to climb, he took his gun and shot some cones down, the noise bringing several more hostile natives to find out what he was doing. Douglas retreated with three cones and some twigs as specimens, but regarded this tree as 'the most princely of the genus, perhaps even the grandest specimens of vegetation',[22] and its discovery as a major achievement of his career. He named it *Pinus lambertiana* in honour of Aylmer Bourke Lambert. Douglas's North American expeditions

Pinus sylvestris.

Scots pine engraved after Ferdinand Bauer for A. B. Lambert's *A Description of the Genus Pinus . . .* (1803–24).

revealed other conifers to Europeans, including Monterey pine, ponderosa or western yellow pine, western white pine, Coulter pine and gray pine. Douglas himself came to an untimely end while collecting in Hawaii. This was a hazard of the plant hunter's life; John Jeffrey (*b.* 1826), discoverer of the Jeffrey pine, vanished in Arizona in 1854. Expeditions to China and Southeast Asia also revealed pine species new to botany, although their impact was less profound on Western consciousness.

Discovery of the plant wealth of the New World, combined with developments in taxonomy, led to a complex tangle of literature on pine trees. The difficulty of dealing with pines was compounded by the number of common names given to individual species of these most useful and ornamental trees; for instance, North American eastern white pine became known as Weymouth pine when first introduced to England, after the first Lord Weymouth, who planted it extensively at Longleat in the early 1700s.[23] The name is still in use, along with about 65 other common names in English, French, Spanish, German, Swedish and other languages. Some are obvious translations (*Weymouths-keifer*); others have local associations (Minnesota white pine) or refer to characteristics important to those who handle them (pumpkin pine, balsam pine), but others (such as the Hungarian *simafenyö*) are impervious to the non-specialist.[24]

Once the genus *Pinus* achieved recognition, botanists succumbed to a desire to divide it into groups, tribes or sections. The resulting forest of botanical literature is one of the most striking and daunting features of the history of pines. It is further complicated by changes in the botanical names given to individual species. The history of naming pines is complex: over time, botanical conventions about assigning names, the emphasis laid on particular aspects of the plants and the overall philosophy of classification have all changed to an extent remarked upon with despair even by botanists.[25]

A multiplicity of terms runs through the literature, usage and meaning depending on the author, date and purpose of the work. Species were demoted to subspecies, or re-elevated or divided in two because observations showed them to be sufficiently different; some were renamed in the twentieth century, when the International Rules of Botanical Nomenclature were changed, rendering previous names invalid. Scientific understanding of the genus is still incomplete: in the nineteenth century, when the desire to divide into subgroups took root, it was only half-realized. Not only were new species being discovered, but also the natural variability displayed by pines according to genetics and habitat was only just emerging.

Tree species that could be assigned to other genera were removed from the genus *Pinus* by major and logical subtractions. In 1754 the Scottish botanist Philip Miller (1691–1771) recognized firs (genus *Abies*) and larch (genus *Larix*) as separate, but spruces (genus *Picea*) were not separated out until 1824.[26] Separating genera was one thing, but botanists continued to subdivide them. The path to present-day opinions on pines is littered with discarded proposals and analyses.

Criteria used by botanists to identify and classify pines were based on observable morphology – number of leaves in each bundle, shape of cones, texture of bark and more subtle features to do with microscopic and internal structure. From the mid-eighteenth century, when the French botanist Henri-Louis Duhamel (1700–1782) proposed a simple system based on leaves, botanists arranged and rearranged the species as the genus steadily increased in size. 'No difficulty exists in the circumspection of the genus Pinus', wrote George Engelmann (1809–1884);

> floral characters unite with vegetative to establish it so firmly and so plainly that nobody fails to recognise the species belonging to it. But when we come to analyze and to group 60 or 70 species of pines which are known to us, we find that they appear so similar that all attempts to arrange them satisfactorily have failed.[27]

Engelmann was extremely thorough in his observations and divided the genus into two sections that he named *strobus* and *pinaster*.

Observations by late nineteenth-century botanists about the internal structure of pine leaves led to another division when Bernhard Koehne (1848–1918) also divided the genus into two sections: *haploxylon* for those with needles that contained one fibrovascular bundle (the tissue that conducts water and nutrients), *diploxylon* for those with two. These terms became important and influential. They

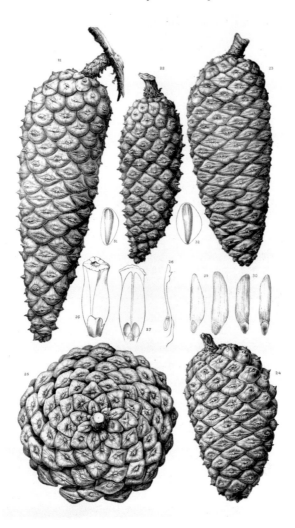

Cone of slash pine (*P. elliottii*) drawn by Paulus Roetter for George Engelmann's
Revision of the Genus Pinus *and Description of 'P. elliottii'* (1880).

were used by botanists and foresters for much of the twentieth century,
until changes in the International Code of Botanical Nomenclature
rendered them invalid, although the terms haploxyl and diploxyl are
still used colloquially.[28] But many terms – *haploxylon, diploxylon, bifoliis,
australes, parryana, Ducampopinus* – are still enshrined in the literature of
pine trees to trap and confuse.

Eastern white pine (*P. strobus*) engraved after Ferdinand Bauer for A. B. Lambert's
A Description of the Genus 'Pinus' . . . (1803–24).

The numerous systems proposed divided the genus into two
(sometimes three) subgenera, in turn divided into sections and sub-
sections. The problem was – and to some extent remains – in the
observable characteristics used for classification for sections. 'Some
of the characteristics differentiating one system always interfere with

those differentiating another', observed Aljos Farjon.[29] The concept of sections is important when considering species hybridization, as the majority of pine species will only hybridize within their own sub-section. Botanists still disagree over whether some pines constitute species, subspecies or merely variants, and over the best way to organize them into sections.

Morphology, location and environment identify individual pine species but do not give definitive groupings. The interaction of genotype (the inherited potential) and phenotype (the actual development of the tree as dictated by environmental factors) leads to much variability in some species. Due to convergent evolution, especially for traits such as large, edible seeds distributed by birds, unrelated species separated by wide distances, mountain ranges or oceans can appear superficially very similar.

DNA analysis has helped unwind some details, but it is expensive and relationships between genes and, for instance, shapes of cones, can only be inferred. A more recent method known as clade analysis, studying the relationships of characters derived from common ancestors, produces branching diagrams (similar to 'tree-of-life' diagrams), which indicate relationships. This has led to more definitive ideas about how to subdivide the genus. From this mass of observation, description, data and conjecture accumulated over the past 250 years, the most consistent point that has emerged is the division of genus *Pinus* into two distinct subgenera,[30] now known as subgenus *Strobus* (one vascular bundle per leaf), and subgenus *Pinus* (two vascular bundles per leaf). These are also sometimes colloquially referred to, at least in the USA, as soft or white pines (*Strobus*) and hard or yellow pines (*Pinus*) due to general differences in the wood. The idea of splitting the genus into two separate genera has been mentioned. Because this would require a change of botanical name for every species in the new genus, it remains only an idea – even taxonomists intent on order are not immune to the prospect of derision from their colleagues. Pines remain resistant to the attempts of botanists to tidy them up.

three

Pitch, Turpentine and Rosin

P
ines exude resin that is sticky, aromatic and honey-like. It is a
mixture of solid rosin and liquid turpentine. Produced by the
trees to seal wounds and eject foreign matter, it is viscous and
highly flammable. On the trees it appears in drips and flows; on cones
it oozes in flecks or shows as tear-like drips. When fresh it is glisten-
ingly transparent; as it ages, it becomes milky, looking a little like
candle wax. Resin exposed to the air hardens through evaporation
and oxidation. Other conifers also produce resin, but pines are an
especially rich source. Small amounts can be scraped from naturally
occurring flows, but at some point in the distant past, probably repeat-
edly in different times and places, the idea of deliberately wounding
the trees to increase the flow began.

In China, from an early date, physicians held complex beliefs
about pine resin, *sung chih*, and its relationship to a fungus, *fu ling*
(*Polyporus cocos*), which grows on the roots of pines. The fungus was
thought to be the result of pine resin flowing into the ground and
remaining there for a thousand years, and was considered to be an elixir
of immortality.[1] In ancient Greece the pitys pine was sacred to both
Poseidon, god of the sea, and Dionysus, god of wine. This was not only
because pines produced timber for ships and gave resin or pitch to
preserve them and their tackle, but also because their resin was used
for sealing porous wine vessels and mixed with the wine itself. There
is a hint that resin or pitch may have been more important than
timber in relation to pine trees in the ancient Mediterranean world.

Woodcut illustration for Sebastian Münster's *Cosmographia* (1544–52) showing a pine tree with a collecting box for resin at the roots.

A treaty of the fourth century BC between the Macedonian king and the cities of Chalcidice grants the latter the rights for products from Macedonian forests, mentioning pitch before timber.[2] Pitch is recorded in Old English as *pic*, in Middle English as *picche* or *pisch*, and in continental Europe as *pic, pi, pek* or *peh* in Germanic languages on the North Sea littoral. Well away from the European mainland, the Old Icelandic word was *bik*, and in Eastern Europe related words were recorded in Slavonic languages. Pitch was evidently both sought after and widely travelled.

The early link between pine trees and maritime travel is still apparent in the English expression 'naval stores' to describe the industry that extracts pine products. The phrase originally included cordage (ropes), wood for masts, spars and planks, and pine tar or pitch, but by the nineteenth century it meant pine resin from living trees, the turpentine and rosin distilled from it, and pitch or tar extracted from dead pinewood.[3]

As in all things to do with pine trees, the English vocabulary is fluid. Resin is sometimes called turpentine, gum (especially in the USA) and pitch. Pitch can indicate resin extracted from cut or dead pinewood by heat, also called tar. Rosin, in early texts, is sometimes used to indicate resin. Usage is hopelessly confused, reflecting the great utility of these items in a world without the fossil fuel products now used instead.

Resin, technically oleoresin, is defined as 'a non-aqueous solution of resin acids dissolved in a terpene hydrocarbon oil'.[4] It has excellent adhesive qualities, as anyone who has had to remove it knows (it can be removed from the skin by rubbing in a little fat or oil). In the nineteenth-century turpentine industry of North Carolina, the men working with resin got so much of it on their overalls that the cloth became stiff; unable to fold the overalls, they left them standing in the corner of the cabin at night.[5] Although the word gum is often used in the USA for pine resin, this is inaccurate (gum is water soluble).

Pitch, anciently associated with pine trees, is defined in the *Oxford English Dictionary* as

> a sticky, resinous, black or dark brown substance, hard when cold and semiliquid when hot, that is obtained as a residue from the distillation of wood tar or turpentine and is used for caulking the seams of ships, protecting wood from moisture, etc.

This substance was also referred to as tar, a word traced back to AD 700 in Anglo-Saxon sources, where *teru* or *teoru* were equated with

Latin *resina*. Like the word pitch, tar seems to have had an Indo-European root (this source from the *Oxford English Dictionary*). Pitch and tar are confusing, the words sometimes being used interchangeably, and pitch could refer to a product that had received further heat treatment by boiling. From the earliest records onwards, the word tar was also applied to mineral pitch or bitumen, the sense in which it is now more commonly used. Pine pitch and pine tar have an aroma that is slightly astringent, woody and chemical, but not unpleasant. They have left a lingering smell along quaysides and in sail lofts all along the Western European coast, and the extreme darkness of these products has given English the expression 'pitch-black' for moonless nights and lightless cellars.

Crude resin tapped from living trees was also called turpentine. When distilled it became known as oil of turpentine, and according to the *Oxford English Dictionary* this was

> a volatile oil, contained in the wood, bark, leaves and other parts of coniferous trees, and usually prepared by distilling crude turpentine. There are many varieties according to the source, which, although all having the same formula, $C_{10}H_{16}$, vary in their physical and more especially their optical properties.

Unless otherwise indicated, in this chapter the word 'turpentine' is used to indicate the distilled product. Often abbreviated to 'turps' in English, it combines with linseed oil to produce the characteristic odour of an oil painter's studio – an evocative, never-to-be-forgotten smell. Mineral-derived white spirit is frequently substituted for less-exalted purposes.

Distilling turpentine leaves a clear, solid, pale gold residue in the still. This became known as rosin, a word ultimately derived from Latin *rēsina*, resin (according to the *Oxford English Dictionary*), making the discussion about pine products somewhat circular. Rosin was used to indicate resin by some early modern authors, who used an alternative, now-archaic term, *colophony* (from Colophon, an Ionian island), for this residue. Such a tangle of vocabulary can only indicate that these substances were enormously useful and sought after by people often remote from the area of production. Perhaps for those who lived far from their origin, they had mysterious and slightly magical associations as natural products of forests in distant lands.

As part of his *Enquiry into Plants*, Theophrastus recorded two methods of extraction. Resin could be obtained by tapping living trees such as silver fir and Aleppo pine, a process that, he noted, eventually weakened them. Quality varied according to the aspect of the tree, the finest and purest resin coming from trees growing in a sunny position and facing north. They yielded less in dry weather. Resin was 'carried about in baskets, and so acquires the more solid form which we know'.[6] The second extraction method recorded how the Macedonians and Syrians made pitch by fire using cut or dead wood. A piece of ground was levelled, making a slope for the pitch to run towards the middle. Then cloven logs were placed 'in an arrangement like that used by the charcoal-burners', upright in a pile 180 cubits round by 50 or 60 high (more if the wood was very resinous). The pile was covered with timber, then earth, and fire was kindled through a gap, which was then closed. The smouldering pile was kept covered with earth 'and a conduit is prepared for the pitch right through the pile, so that it may flow off into a hole at about fifteen cubits off'. It burned for two days and nights, after which the pitch stopped flowing. 'All this time they keep watch and do not go to rest, in case the fire should come through; and they offer sacrifice and keep holiday, praying that the pitch my be abundant and good.'[7] This method of extracting pine pitch or tar was later called 'dry distillation', and became widely known. Pomet recorded that pine tar 'is generally brought to us [in France] from Denmark, Norway, Finland and Swedeland; but there is much of it made in New-England, Virginia, Carolina and other Parts of Florida',[8] and that 'black pitch' was a mixture of tar and resin, the best coming from Stockholm. In New England in the eighteenth century, North Carolina became known as the 'Tar Heel' State because of its association with pitch production. Around the end of the seventeenth century, John Evelyn described laying knots from decayed wood on hearths 'after the very same manner as our colliers do their wood for charcoal' in a 'kind of rude distillation'.[9] The method was simple but tedious. It could also be hazardous, as vents made in the cover of the heap – intentionally or otherwise – sometimes needed sealing, with the chance that a worker (or slave in the North American colonies) might suffer burns or even fall into the kiln.

Sweden produced the best pitch. In the early twentieth century, a 'dale', a pitch-producing kiln as used in Sweden, was funnel-shaped and built on a slope, with a spout at the lower end and the interior lined with clay, iron or thick cardboard. The Swedes prepared the trees by barking them from the ground to a height of about 2.5 m, leaving only a narrow strip on the north side that kept the tree alive until the next year. Then they felled them, and the bases, now full of resin, were dried over the summer. The resinous stumps were stacked on the dale and the whole was covered with brushwood and peat. The burning brushwood was carefully controlled so that the pinewood did not flare up, but merely yielded a pitch that was high in turpentine and much in demand. Dry distillation was inefficient but gave a good product; it was still used to a limited extent to produce high-quality pitch in Sweden in the early twentieth century.[10]

Pitch was a variable product. Anciently, Theophrastus recorded that the people of Mount Ida considered pitch (resin) from their local pine to be 'more abundant, blacker, sweeter and generally more fragrant' when raw than that of 'the fir of the seashore', but it contained more 'watery matter', so the amount reduced more when it was boiled down.

Pliny the Elder (AD 23–79) also described pitch produced in various places from different kinds of tree, including a 'spruce' found in Bruttium (southern Italy; possibly a pine formerly known as *Pinus brutia*, now considered a variant of Aleppo pine). He recorded that the early flow of pitch was collected separately, and in Syria was known as cedar oil. Subsequent, thicker pitch was collected in bronze cauldrons

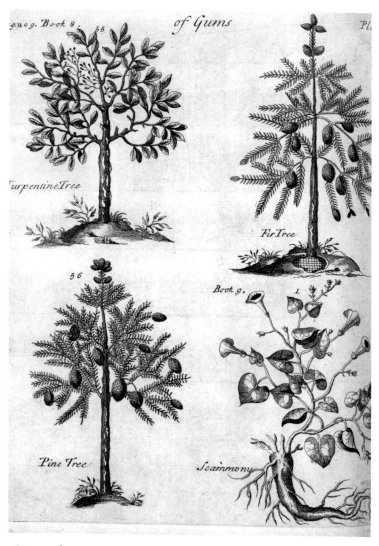

Pine tree, fir tree, turpentine tree: an illustration to Pierre Pomet's *A Compleat History of Druggs* (1737).

and mixed with vinegar to coagulate it. Known as Bruttium pitch, it had a reddish colour and was more viscous and greasier. Pitch could be heated in oak barrels using hot stones; it was evidently solid, as it could be ground up like flour. Cooked gently with water and clarified, it took on a red colour and was known as distilled pitch, although

Mosaic, late 2nd or early 3rd century AD, from St Romain en Gal, showing two
farmworkers coating the inside of porous pottery jars with pine pitch.

this was usually made from inferior resin. Pliny also mentions a special 'intoxication resin', rarely found except in a few places in the
foothills of the Italian Alps. It was made of the 'untreated flower of
resin' and thin, short chips of wood, crushed and steeped in boiling
water until melted. This somewhat mysterious product apparently had
medicinal applications.[11]

Columella (AD 4–*c*. 70), the Roman writer on agriculture, mentions
several different kinds of pitch, including Bruttian pitch, Nemeturican
pitch from Liguria and pitch of the Allobroges from the Savoy region
of the French Alps. *Rasis* was 'a kind of crude pitch', for which he gives
no provenance. They clearly had different qualities, but he says nothing
about the trees with which they were associated.[12]

Pitch is an extraordinarily useful substance. It has anti-microbial and insecticidal properties, as well as the ability to set solid and form water-impermeable barriers, and makes a good adhesive. The ancient Egyptians used some form of pitch (possibly from pine trees) in the mummification process. The precise origin of resins used in the process is unknown, but Pliny wrote that the initial flow of pitch 'has such strength that in Egypt they make use of it for embalming human corpses'.[13] Recent research indicates that this is probably true: analysis of resins from Egyptian mummies has shown that tree resins, some of which were probably from pines, were present.

As a barrier to liquids, a preservative and a flavouring, pitch was frequently used in the ancient world during wine production. Columella had much to say on this subject. Ordinary pitch was used for waterproofing wine jars. The jars sunk into the ground were heated with burning iron torches, the old pitch was scraped, and new pitch was poured in and spread with a brush and wooden ladle to coat the insides. Jars that were above ground were cured in the sun for several days before being turned upside down above a fire that heated them until they were too hot to touch. Then hot pitch was poured in and the jars were rolled until every bit of the inside was covered.[14]

Purified pitch mixed with spices or seawater was for preserving the wine itself. Columella's instructions for purifying Nemeturican pitch are complex. First it was washed three times with lye (alkali made from wood ash). Then Bruttian pitch and 'old seawater' (partially evaporated and stored) were added, and the mixture was left uncovered in the sun 'during the rising of the dog-star'.[15] It was stirred periodically until all the seawater had evaporated. Nemeturican pitch on its own could be used, mixed with warm seawater that had been reduced by boiling. When the pitch had settled the water was poured off, more was mixed in and it was stirred until it became bright red in colour. The pitch was allowed to stand in the sun for fourteen days, then mixed, first with a little fermenting wine must, then into the main body of the wine. Columella also recommended that powdered pitch, sometimes combined with spices, should be mixed into wine as a preservative. Purification may have been an attempt to reduce the distinctive flavor of the pitch. The Romans, it seems, did not want their wine to taste of pitch: Columella says that the flavour of the preservative should not be noticeable, 'for that drives away the purchaser'.[16]

Pitch was still recommended as a preservative for wine in *Geoponika* (a tenth-century book of agricultural instructions compiled in Constantinople), first being washed with lye and then mixed with other resins, perfumes and spices. Wine jars were still pitched inside. Some people added wax to the pitch, but others counselled against this 'because the wine will be astringent, and thus more readily turn vinegary'.[17] *Retsina*, flavoured with pine resin, is still produced in Greece when all practical necessity for it has ceased. Reactions are mixed among those unused to it, with many regarding it as an acquired taste.

Pitch-coated or pitch-sealed jars were also used for preserving fresh fruit for winter; bunches of grapes (any overripe ones carefully snipped off), pears and apples are all mentioned in this context. *Geoponika* also contains instructions for this. Fruit should be stored in pitched wooden boxes filled with dry pine or fir sawdust. The stems of pears should be tipped with pitch before they are hung up to keep (pears with their stems dipped in a red sealing compound are still sold in Italian markets); in a jar of dried figs, a few dipped in pitch and interspersed among the rest would prevent them from going mouldy.

Numerous other minor uses were recorded. Pitch mixed with bull's bile or *amorge* (the bitter, watery by-product of olive pressing) was used to deter ants; mixed with the juice of squirting cucumber, it killed bedbugs. Medicinal uses often related to treating skin lesions, sometimes in humans, but especially in animals. *Geoponika* mentions pitch mixed with sulphur as a treatment for mange in oxen, with olive oil and ash for treating cuts, or with salt as a poultice for suppurating wounds on oxen. For humans, a recipe for a mixture of honey, liquid pitch, oil, butter and pig fat against the cough is listed.[18] Pitch was used to coat bronze and other metals to prevent tarnishing. It was used as a dressing for minor wounds on sheep incurred during shearing. For vain men it made a useful depilatory, and for artists it was a source of pigment. Such uses are also apparent in Chinese literature. From antiquity, the resin of Masson pine (*P. massoniana*) was known as a treatment for skin problems caused by parasites, and later Chinese works also listed the twigs, leaves, flowers, cones, bark and root as useful for their insecticidal properties.[19]

As a sticky substance that catches fire easily, pitch was useful in warfare. There are records of its use both in the classical European world and in ancient China, where it was recorded that a primitive but probably deadly weapon in the form of a flame-thrower was composed of gunpowder, pitch and various noxious substances. Flame-throwers became known later in medieval Europe, and were called fire lances in English.[20]

In North America native peoples used pine pitch as an adhesive. One of the most striking and spectacular examples of this use appears in the exquisite turquoise mosaics made by the Aztecs in the time just before the Spanish conquest. Shaped over wood carved into discs, animals and knives, and over other forms, including masks in which a

Pears on sale in an Italian market in 2009. Their stems are sealed in the manner recommended 1,000 years ago.

Sanford R. Gifford,
*Birch Canoe of the Mic
Mac's Nova Scotia*,
1859, pencil on
paper. These fragile,
light boats were
constructed from
sheets of birch bark,
using pine tar both
as an adhesive and a
waterproofer for the
seams.

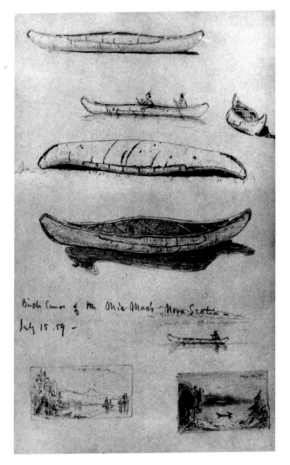

human skull was sometimes used as a base, the turquoise was glued
to the base material with resin. Another use was to glue stone arrow-
heads to wooden shafts. Pine pitch was used for waterproofing baskets
and porous pottery.

In the seventeenth century, John Evelyn still recorded rosins,
liquid pitch and tar as having uses for 'Arthritic and Pulmonic Infections', and for plasters after surgery. Mechanics (tradesmen generally)
had 'innumerable uses' for them.[21] Pomet said that pitch

cures all Sorts of Scabs, Itch, Tettars, Ringworms and other
Vices of the Skin. *Tar* is better than pitch because in boiling

Extraordinarily useful: pine pitch and tar were a major Swedish export, travelling the world for many purposes; here it is packaged for sheep-shearers in Australia.

the Pitch loses the more subtle and firey parts, and therefore it is proper for Coughs, Phthysicks, Hoarseness, and other Humours that fall upon the Lungs.[22]

Tar and beeswax made a plaster good against the gout and old aches and pains. Minor uses of pitch continued to display an eclectic nature down almost to the present day: as stiffening and waterproofing for both tarpaulins and nineteenth-century miners' felt hats; as a foaming agent that helped separate tin ore from rock in tin mines; and as sizing for the wooden boards used by oil painters, a method favoured by the eighteenth-century English artist George Stubbs. Even now, a pot of pine pitch under the name 'Stockholm Tar' is part of every farmer's medical armoury for treating wounds and minor infections among livestock, and for grooms and farriers in the care of horses.

Pine products, especially pitch and tar, had an enormous part to play in seafaring and the politics of naval supremacy. Perhaps the earliest reference to their use in this context is biblical: 'Make thee an ark of gopher wood; rooms thou shalt make in the ark, and shalt pitch it within and without with pitch' (King James Bible, Genesis 6:14). The story of Noah's Ark is only slightly spoiled by the possibility that bitumen was intended (Noah being closer to sources of this than the translators of the King James Bible were), but pine pitch was obviously known from early times. Prehistoric boats and ships built of wood leave few physical traces – and allowance has to be made for the possibility of even more fragile craft of withies and animal skins, or birch bark, perhaps waterproofed with pitch, now represented by Irish curraghs of canvas and bitumen, and Welsh coracles. Native North Americans certainly knew its value. David Douglas recorded canoes made of birch bark, with seams 'neatly gummed with the resin of pine'.[23]

Pliny records that the first flow, the liquid pitch, was used for treating ship's tackle, but the wooden ships of the classical world were constructed in a way that meant they did not need caulking. Pitch was still applied to their hulls as a preservative. This gave rise to a product known to the Greeks as 'live pitch', which was scraped off sea-going ships and mixed with wax. Considered much more efficacious for all applications in which pitch was normally used,[24] it went by a curious name transmitted to the early modern world as zopissa, still evidently sought after in some form in the seventeenth century. Pomet said:

> There is another black Pitch, which the Ancients call Zopissa, and is properly what the Mariners call *Pitch* and *Tar*, and which serves them to pitch their Vessels with. This *Zopissa* is a Composition of black Pitch, Rosin, Suet and Tar, melted together; and this is what is sold for true Ship Pitch, and us'd as such by the Apothecaries in their Compositions where this is required.[25]

Whatever its role in seafaring in the ancient world, pitch became increasingly important in late medieval and early modern Europe, as sea travel in ships caulked and sealed with pitch extended. Two kinds, one called 'schippe picche', were mentioned by the late thirteenth-century English monk Bartholomaeus Anglicus in his compendium *On the Properties of Things (De Proprietatibus Rerum)*. Ships were treated to 'kepe yat water schal nought come in to ye schippe' (*Oxford English Dictionary*). He also said that there was much pitch to be found in Greece. Pitch sealed the caulked seams and preserved the timbers and rope work of ships. In the Royal Naval Museum at Portsmouth there is an undistinguished length of rope, frayed at one end, dark brown in colour and partially coated with a slightly greasy black substance. From the time when Henry VIII's favourite warship, *Mary Rose*, sank in 1545 until her wreck was excavated in the 1980s, this lay anaerobically sealed under sediment on the seabed, preserving, remarkably, both the pitch and a smell of pine tar.

Hot pine tar being used to seal oakum-caulked seams on the wooden deck of the flagship *Niagara*.

In the human history of pine trees, the period of colonial expansion from the fifteenth-century voyages of discovery through to the development of steam power and iron ships emerges as a time when pine trees and their products played an essential part in economics and politics, especially in a period of shifting alliances between maritime countries during the eighteenth and nineteenth centuries. Pine pitch or tar, and turpentine and rosin, all essential for wooden ships, increased in importance as the naval power of the Western European trading nations grew, to the extent that they became both an important source of revenue for producer areas and a political bargaining point. In early modern Europe, barrels of Swedish pitch were traded around the North Sea to countries such as the Netherlands and England, whose depleted native pine forests could no longer supply their own. It was a cash crop, and each type was named for the district of northern Sweden from which it originated. Pitch became a trading monopoly of the Wood Tar Company of North Sweden, founded in 1648, the sole export privileges granted by the Swedish crown.[26] Because of this, high-quality pitch became known as Stockholm Tar (in contrast to pitch of lesser quality produced in Finland and Russia). This monopoly increased the price of pine tar, doubling it between 1689 and 1699.[27] Alliances between countries, cost and tax regimes influenced the use of Swedish pitch in Europe between the seventeenth and nineteenth centuries, as did new sources of naval stores.

The English marked out North American forests as a source of naval stores from the start, and the 1704 Act for Encouraging the Importation of Naval Stores from America allowed the Navy to pay bounties on tar, pitch, turpentine, rosin, hemp and wood for masts and spars. In time, this allowed the British to become exporters of naval stores to other European countries and drove down the price of Swedish products.[28] During the eighteenth century the vast stands of longleaf pine growing on land unsuited to agriculture in North Carolina became a valuable source of resin products, replacing Sweden and its neighbours. Later in the century, politics in the form of the American Revolution intervened, and the British were forced back

RETRIBUTION; — Tarring & Feathering; — or — The Patriots Revenge.
———— "Nay & you'll stop Our Mouths, beware Your Own!"

James Gillray, *Retribution; Tarring & Feathering; or The Patriots Revenge*, hand-coloured
etching, 1795. William Pitt, Prime Minister and chief agent of the war against
Revolutionary France, is being tarred and feathered by radical sympathizers Charles
James Fox (with tar on a mop) and the playwright turned MP Richard Brinsley
Sheridan (tipping feathers out of a French Revolutionary 'Liberty cap'). This
was a highly visible, and possibly very ancient means of showing disgrace.

Detail of standing rigging from HMS *Victory*. All such rope work on sailing ships was protected against seawater with pine tar.

to Baltic supplies at a time when they were involved in the Napoleonic Wars, much of which were fought at sea.

The demand for pine tar must have been immense. HMS *Victory*, Nelson's flagship at the Battle of Trafalgar in 1805, carried 42 km of rigging. Of this, about 10 per cent was 'standing rigging' treated with pine tar as a preservative. *Victory* was one of the largest ships of the time, but pine products were a necessity for all ships, whether men o' war, the merchant fleets of East and West Indiamen, or innumerable smaller trading and fishing craft, not only in Britain but in all the maritime nations of northern Europe, the Mediterranean and the Americas.

Control of supply through production or trade was a source of political power. Pitch was essential for waterproofing and preserving wood and rope, and all ships carried a pitch kettle among their gear. Sailors boiled pine tar to condense it further before coating the rigging and using it to seal caulked seams between the planks of a ship's hull (giving British sailors their nickname of Jack Tars), and waterproofed canvas sheets to make tarpaulins. The demand for pitch and tar only eased when gradually, through the nineteenth century, the development of iron-hulled, steam-driven ships to replace wooden sailing ships resulted in less need for it, and tar from coal provided competition. At the same time, new markets developed for pine products, especially turpentine and rosin.

The resin for turpentine was always extracted from living trees in pre-industrial times. Originally appearing in English as *terebentine*, the word turpentine derives from terebinth (genus *Pistacia*), a tree unrelated to pine and native to the eastern Mediterranean, whose highly valued resin it originally denoted. This is still available as Cyprian or Chian turpentine, from the island of Chios. By the seventeenth century, turpentine was also a name given to products from conifers including pines, firs and larches. Like pitch and tar, turpentine was a variable product whose qualities to some extent depended on area and producer. Pomet listed turpentine of Chio (terebinth) and

> the *Turpentine* from the Pine Wood and the *Bordeaux Turpentine*. There are several others besides these to be met with in the Shops, which are nothing else but false Names given to them, according to their Adulterations.[29]

Then there were 'true Venice turpentine', Cyprus and Pisa turpentine, and Strasbourg turpentine, which was frequently sold in Holland. Turpentine from southwest France was apparently not of the highest quality; it was 'the common *Turpentine*, to which some give the name of *Bayonne*, or *Bordeaux Turpentine*. This is white, and thick as Honey, and comes most from *Bordeaux*, *Nantz* or *Rouen*.' It was made from *galipot*, a 'white hard rosin [resin]' exuded from pines and came from Guyenne, a loosely defined province of southwest France in pre-revolutionary times.[30]

In 1831, John Davies recorded numerous types of turpentine – common turpentine from *P. sylvestris*, Bordeaux turpentine from *P. maritima*, Strasbourg turpentine from '*P. picea* . . . silver fir tree' and Venice turpentine from larches. He also recorded two varieties probably unavailable when Pomet was writing 150 years earlier: one he

Georg Dionysius Ehret, *Study of a Marsh Pine with Two Cones*, 1725–70, watercolour and body colour on vellum.

called *Terebintha canadensis* (from American silver fir), and 'American tur-pentine, furnished abundantly by the *Pinus palustris, Lin, P. australis*, Michaux, a tree growing principally in the southern states'.[31]

Conifer turpentine was produced by true distillation, a colour-less, aromatic liquid much used as a solvent, technically known as oil of turpentine. Pomet said that it should be clear and white as Water, of a strong penetrating Smell; yet this is a mischievous Commodity, and great Cheats in it, besides the risque of Fire, and the little Profit there is got by it, which is the Reason why so many People will not deal in it.[32]

Nicholas Mirov, whose work involved much analysis of the chemistry of the volatile components of pine resin, commented that in the twentieth century the word turpentine was rather loosely applied to the distillate and that the concentrations varied according to the producer. Turpentine was, and remains, expensive.

The point at which resin from living trees was first distilled to make turpentine is unknown. The origins of distillation for alcohol lie in the ritual uses of wine by Dionysian cults in the late centuries BC,[33] but the development of the pot still and worm (for cooling, both essential in the distillation of turpentine and many other substances) were essentially products of the alchemical investigations of the early Middle Ages. The search for the elixir of life led to many discoveries. It seems reasonable to assume that tree resins, like numerous other organic and inorganic substances, were used in these experiments.

Pot stills remained in use into the nineteenth century, and using them was dangerous. Temperature control was crucial; the distiller had a narrow band between 363°F and 392°F (184–200°C) that gave optimum results. If the mass cooled during distilling, vapour trapped in it resulted in a danger of it boiling over; heating too fast created too much vapour. Both could lead to disastrous fires. The process depended on the skill and experience of the distiller, who assessed quality by looking at the distillate, and listened to the sounds at the end of the worm to estimate how the resin was boiling.[34] Adding water to resin improved the process. Turpentine distillation moved into the industrial age in the mid-nineteenth century with introductions such as thermometers for use in the stills, agreed standards and the design of a continuous process still.

Afbeelding van een Terpentyn-olie-Branderij. Figure d'une Maison ou l'on fait de l'Huile de en zyn Pakhuijs met terpentyn beleidt op de Terebentine, avec son Magazin; situee sur le Passeerders graft, welke branderij ontstak en Passeerders graft ala quelle le Feu se prit, et geblust wierdt den 17 December 1683. fut eteint le 17 Decembre 1683.

Jan van Vianen after Jan van der Heyden, *Ruins of a turpentine-oil distillery on the Passeerdersgracht in Amsterdam, 17th December 1683*, c. 1690, etching and engraving. Fire and explosion were ever-present hazards for the owners of turpentine distilleries.

The turpentine industry led to a remarkable exploitation of the native pine forests of the southeastern USA in the nineteenth century, starting with the long-leaf pine forests of North Carolina. Since the eighteenth century the 'piney woods' had been exploited for wood, pitch and tar. By the 1830s oil of turpentine was more profitable, and the industry expanded with improvements in both transport and technology. It was pursued in a manner destructive to the forests:[35] tapping the trees by 'boxing'. This involved removing some of the bark and sapwood where a prominent root left the tree to make a hollow in which the resin collected. Above this, the bark and sapwood were partially removed in a distinctive pattern of downward-pointing chevrons extending up the trunk for a few centimetres. Down this 'cat's face', with its downward-pointing, shallow 'V' cuts, the resin oozed from the damaged wood and collected in the box. The gum, as it was called locally, was scooped into barrels, taken to local centres and distilled for turpentine. Dried resin scraped from the face of the trees was also sold, but 'scrape' was lower quality than liquid resin.

The work was poorly paid and only those who controlled large areas of trees made much money from it. 'Turpentining' in the thinly populated pine woods initially depended on slave labour. Frederick Law Olmsted (1822–1903), a journalist who worked in North Carolina, remarked that

> Negroes employed in this branch of industry seemed to me unusually intelligent and cheerful. Decidedly they are superior in every moral and intellectual respect to the great mass of people inhabiting the turpentine forest.[36]

They did much collecting and transporting of resin, a sticky, dirty task, as well as a lonely one. Poor whites also worked in turpentining – some were squatters who valued the isolation and opportunities for small-scale cropping the woods offered.

Quantities involved were vast, turpentine was relatively valuable and the industry had a huge impact as transport improved. The pine trees were worked to exhaustion by the late nineteenth century. Less destructive systems of extraction were trialled unsuccessfully, and extracting pitch and turpentine from stumps became futile when the stumps themselves were all consumed. Lumbermen began to compete with naval stores producers for the trees. The industry depleted the basis for its own existence and migrated south into vast tracts of untapped pines that still flourished in Alabama, Mississippi and

A 'cat's face' chevron pattern as a partially healed wound on a pine trunk, showing that the tree was once tapped for resin.

Florida. In North Carolina today, only about 3,900 ha of old-growth longleaf pine remain from an original range of 37 million.[37]

A less destructive method of turpentine extraction developed in nineteenth-century France. Here, forests of maritime pine had been planted to stabilize sand dunes in Les Landes, southwest of Bordeaux, in the eighteenth century, a policy encouraged by Napoleon and subsequent administrators. The resin was collected by making a small incision at the base of a tree, and a gutter guided the flow into metal or clay collecting vessels. More expensive and labour-intensive, but less damaging to the trees, this method produced a higher-grade product. Eventually, the system was adopted in the eastern USA, but by the early twentieth century France dominated production of naval stores using resin from Les Landes and pitch from Aleppo pine forests

95

in its colony of Algeria. European countries including the USSR, Greece, Spain and Portugal also developed as sources of supply. Tapping pines for resin is labour intensive. By the 1990s, production had moved to South American countries using introduced pine species such as slash pine. Increasing costs there led to a move to Southeast Asia using Sumatran pine, and China, where several species are tapped, most importantly Masson pine. Chir pine is also used in India. Of the 'traditional' Western producer countries, only Portugal remained important in the world markets, although some countries, such as Russia, were producers that consumed almost all production domestically.[38]

Turpentine was almost as useful as pitch. Historically, it was much employed as a medicine despite being poisonous. 'All the Turpentines,' said Pomet,

> yield a great deal of Oil, and volatile acid, or essential Salt. They are very aperitive, proper for the Stone, and for Colicks, Ulcers of the Kidney and Bladder, Retention of Urine and Gonorrhoea . . . It gives the Urine a Violet Smell, and creates sometimes a Pain in the Head.[39]

Samuel Pepys, who suffered from kidney stones, was one person who found turpentine a useful medicine. On 1 January 1664, he recorded that he talked at dinner with a doctor 'whose discourse did please me very well, about the disease of the stone, above all things extolling Turpentine, which he told me how it may be taken in pills with great ease. There was brought to table a hot pie made of a swan.'[40]

Turpentine also had dangers. John Davies warned that,

> Adminstered internally in large doses, it produces, in the first instance, nausea, vomiting and abundant alvine evacuations; afterwards, it is absorbed, and it produces a lively excitement throughout the whole economy, as is evinced by the frequency of the pulse, the heat and redness of the skin, cephelagia, vertigoe, &c.

A pot still for turpentine in Florida, 1930s. The owner is facing the 'gooseneck', the tube leading the distillate from the top of the still out through the wall into a coiled condensing tube.

Like others before him, Davies recommended turpentine for urinary tract problems, among other things:

> It is employed with great advantage in the last period of chronic catarrhs of the bladder . . . it is frequently applied externally to cleanse wounds and ulcers, and it enters into the composition of numerous salves and irritating plasters.[41]

Another important use of turpentine was as a solvent. House painters, artists, carriage makers and furniture makers were among those who had cause to use it. It helped to thin oil-based paint and to clean brushes that had been used with it. For those needing varnish – such as makers of musical instruments, furniture and artists –

turpentine and pine resin were both part of an armoury of ingredients including many gums, solvents and waxes. The exact nature of
these and the quantities in which they were combined were often
kept secret and could give significant differences, for instance, in the
sound of violins treated with them. Common turpentine (resin) was
used to make printer's ink, and resin and oil of turpentine melted
together was used by farriers to make coarse varnish, 'but this is a
Composition they are forced to make in private or bye Places, for
fear of Fire', noted Pomet.[42] In the mid-nineteenth century, turpentine found new uses as an ingredient of a North American lamp fuel
known as palm oil, and as a solvent in the nascent rubber industry.

Rosin, the residue from turpentine distilling, is clear and sets to
a hard, brittle, amorphous mass that melts easily at relatively low
temperatures. Its colour varies from dark brown and quite opaque
to pale yellow and clear, the finest grade. For many centuries it had
fewer applications than turpentine and its value fluctuated. The most
often quoted use is as a lubricant for the bows of stringed instruments,
a practice that helps the bow grip the strings more easily and gives a
better sound. The larger the instrument, the softer the rosin should
be. Another, less visible nineteenth-century use was as an ingredient
of composition, a chalk-based mixture pressed into wooden forms for
decorative mouldings.

In the early years of turpentine distilling in North Carolina, the
value of rosin was often so low that it was simply discharged onto
waste ground or into lakes. Uses were found for rosin in the making of
varnishes and soaps, but a new and important use evolved in the
1820s. At this time papermakers began to use rosin to size paper and
make it less absorbent, a use that grew as their industry expanded. It
became more valuable and eventually was exported too. Discarded rosin
was exploited for profit from around the end of the American Civil
War well into the twentieth century.[43]

Although pine products still find many of their traditional uses,
for instance as remedies for coughs, other uses have been superseded by
synthetic products developed from oil during the twentieth century.

Some new markets also developed: rosin yielded a product that was used in vinyl discs for the music industry until they were displaced by compact discs in the 1980s.

Experiments, scientific and otherwise, revealed that the chemistry of pine resin varies widely according to the species. It was a major focus of study for Nicolas Mirov, who told of unexpected hazards when resin distilling started in California during the American Civil War. Correct identification of tree species was essential. Ponderosa pine was a species whose resin was safe to distil, but Jeffrey pine, which is very similar in appearance, contains heptane, a highly inflammable hydrocarbon. It is a constituent of petrol, the substance that makes petrol engines 'knock'. The two species were sometimes confused by distillers, and heating a pot still loaded with Jeffrey pine resin was like 'building a fire underneath a gasoline tank'. Mirov provided heptane extracted from Jeffrey pine resin, which was sometimes called the 'gasoline tree', for the development of the octane scale for petrol.[44]

Authors constantly mention the hazards of naval stores. They must have caused many fires, and were perhaps instrumental in one of the most famous conflagrations of all time. In the seventeenth century, London, a major port, contained many chandlers' shops packed with naval stores, which worried John Evelyn. On 5 September 1666, he felt vindicated, writing in his diary:

> The coal and wood-wharfs, and magazines of oil, rosin, &c, did infinite mischief, so as the invective which little before I had dedicated to his Majesty and published, giving warning what might probably be the issue of suffering those shops to be in the City, was looked on as a prophecy.

The Great Fire of London had finally burned itself out, but not before it had consumed, among other things, vast quantities of naval stores.[45]

Methods for extracting pitch, turpentine and other pine derivatives underwent great changes in the late nineteenth century, partly as new papermaking processes developed. Products were first distilled

Pouring rosin into containers to set, France, 1950s.

directly from cut wood, but then became by-products of the pulpwood and paper industries. 'Sulphate naval stores' is the name given to pitch and turpentine extracted from tall oil, an anglicized version of Swedish *tall olja*, pine oil. This is skimmed off during papermaking by the Kraft process (a method of making paper using sodium hydroxide and sodium sulphide). Tall oil is 'a mixture of resin acids and fatty acids (mostly unsaturated), together with unsaponifiables',[46] which can be further processed. Pine oil is, among other things, 'a good emulsifier, an excellent solvent, an effective germicide . . . an effective frothing agent for floating off impurities'.[47] Many benefits are claimed for the Kraft process, including the fact that by-products can be burned to generate power, but it generates a most noxious smell as gaseous sulphur compounds are also produced.

Until recently, gum naval stores produced from resin tapped from living trees were considered better than tall oil products, which often suffered from odour problems and had a tendency to crystallize. Coal-tar distillation, developed in Germany by the mid-seventeenth century, also expanded rapidly after 1845, its derivatives replacing pine products.

Traditional uses of rosin and turpentine — in soap, paper size, paint and varnish — are still important in developing countries, but both products are now also hugely important as raw materials for the chemical industry. They are chemically complex and can be broken down into many constituents. Modern industrial applications of rosin still include sizing paper, and it is also an ingredient in adhesives, printing ink, fluxes, surface coatings on pharmaceutical tablets, chewing gum, synthetic rubber, detergents and chewing gum. Alpha- and beta-pinene extracted from turpentine are used in the synthesis of fragrances, flavours, vitamins and resins. Turpentine is further processed by fractional distillation; components such as citronellol and menthol are used in flavours and fragrances,[48] but it is synthetic pine oil, another derivative, which lends the characteristic pine smell to disinfectant.

four

Pine for Timber and Torches

☙

R ayon is made from pinewood. So are paper and cardboard, chipboard, match wood, dowelling, planking, inexpensive furniture of all descriptions and kitchen fittings. Pine joists hold up floors, pine poles carry telephone wires and pine pallets aid in the handling of goods in warehouses. The wood is used to make boxes and small domestic objects of all kinds. For humans pinewood has meant warmth, light and charcoal. Twigs, leaves, bark and roots have all found applications. Every part of the tree has had a use at some point in one or another culture around the world. The subject is both vast and only patchily charted by writers.

Pine is softwood, a term indicating that it is (mostly) relatively easy to work when compared with hardwoods produced by deciduous trees. The pitch content also acts as a natural preservative, making pinewood resistant to decay. Within the genus *Pinus*, species in subgenus *Strobus* are sometimes colloquially called 'soft pines', and those in subgenus *Pinus* 'hard pines' because of relative differences in their wood – although as with all things to do with pine trees, there are exceptions.

In everyday use the word 'pine' is a generalized term for conifer wood, one that subsumes wood from a multiplicity of species. In 1866, J. Lindley and T. Moore said the word applied 'especially to that of *Pinus strobus*', and that 'Baltic, Riga, Norway, Red, or Memel Pine is the timber of *Pinus sylvestris* as grown in the north of Europe'.[1] The latter was also known as red deal or Christiania deal because it was shipped

Industrial pine: another lorry load of logs delivered to a processing plant.

from the Baltic port of Christiania, now known as Oslo. 'Red wood' is still the British timber trade name for Scots pine, but white 'Baltic pine' is a trade name for Norway spruce (*Picea abies*), also known as white wood.[2] 'Deal' is a word of Germanic origin derived from timber-trade vocabulary (as is 'wainscot') to describe sawn timber. *Deal* related to size, not species, indicating pieces at least 12 ft long, 7 in. wide, and not more than 3 in. thick (approx. 3,660 x 180 x 80 mm). Special end uses, such as masts for ships, required certain attributes, but otherwise pine was pine, a commodity traded from wherever it could be easily extracted.

Numerous trade synonyms evolved for the best-known species of North American and Western European pine. A. B. Lyons, who published a *Dictionary of Plant Names* in 1900, listed, for instance, for longleaf pine:

> Georgia pine, southern or swamp pine, broom pine, Florida or Virgina pine, Georgia or Texas yellow pine, southern or yellow pitch pine, southern hard pine, long-straw pine, turpentine pine, yellow pine, white rosin tree.[3]

E & CO.

...ers of

...lt by Wm. E. DODGE.
...up!

SPRUCE & HEMLOCK

CAMP SCENE.

J. A. VAPP.

TOBYHANNA MILLS, Monroe Co. Pa.
Capacity 12,000,000 Ft. S Case Sup!

LOG DRIVING.

...E MILLS

LUMBER.

Rough or Dressed
delivered by Car or Boat Load
from the Mills on the
Rail Roads & Canals in
New Jersey & Pennsylvania.
or at the Companys Yards.

TIMBER BILLS.
of Pine, Spruce and
Hemlock, cut promptly
to Order.

From TOBYHANNA Mills,
Spruce PILES & SPARS.
Hemlock BARK, Beech,
Birch, Ash & Maple Hardwoods

Best Varieties from MICHIGAN
& CANADA at the Yards.

PACKING BOXES of all
descriptions made promptly
to order at Jersey City & Newark.

36,000,000 Ft. PINE per Annum.

BOOM AT WILLIAMSPORT.

BER.

OAKINGTON Mills, Havre de Grace, Md.
CAPACITY, 15,000,000 Ft.

MES & CO.

LTIMORE, MD.

of the above Ports.

CITY BLOCK.
Baltimore, Md.

Even those in the timber trade despaired of these myriad names. In 1909, the periodical *American Lumberman and Building Products Merchandiser* lamented the confusion over the terms 'Western pine' and 'Western white pine'. Western pine, or Western yellow pine, was *Pinus ponderosa*, but could also be found under the names California white pine, Western white pine, Navajo white pine, Western pine, Panhandle pine, Idaho white pine or even 'famous looking glass pine' in one edition of the journal alone.[4]

Trade names of pine are no easier in the twenty-first century. SPF is an acronym used in the USA, applied to sawn wood sold for general carpentry and utility purposes, and stands for 'Spruce-Pine-Fir'. The distinction between the trees, so carefully worked out by botanists, is concealed again by the demands of the timber industry. From a practical point of view, perhaps identification is not important. From the earliest times, people must have used whatever was to hand, with only woodworkers recognizing special qualities according to species and origin.

Those with a botanical interest seem to have been the people who most commented in writing on the qualities of wood from different species and regions. In *Arboretum et Fruticetum Britannicum*, arboriculturist John Claudius Loudon remarked how Scots pine timber from different locations varied:

> in low situations, where it is a lofty timber tree, the wood on some light, sandy soils is white, almost without resin, and of little duration; while on other soils, of a colder and more substantial nature, it is red, heavy, and of great durability.[5]

By contrast, his description of wood from Swiss stone pine speaks of its generally small size, sweet perfume and soft, fine-grained nature: 'in joinery it is of great value, as it is remarkably easy to be worked . . . The

previous: Advertisement for Dodge & Co, manufacturers of lumber, late 19th century. The North American timber trade ruthlessly exploited vast areas of forest from the early 19th century onwards, using first water and then steam power to aid this.

wood is much used for wainscoting, having not only an agreeable light brown appearance, but retaining its odour.' It carved easily, and the Swiss shepherds 'occupy their leisure hours in carving out of it numerous small curious little figures of men and animals, which they sell in the towns and which have found their way all over Europe.'[6] It was also used for wood turning.

The utility of the pine tree was frequently praised. In the seventeenth century, John Evelyn said it could be used for carving 'for capitals, festoons, nay statues'. He listed numerous other uses: boxes, barrels, shingles for houses and hoops for wine vessels; it was good for scaffolding and had a natural spring useful for coach-builders. Pines also provides kernels and 'for tooth-pickers even the very leaves are commended'. He also said that it was good 'for piles to superstruct in boggy grounds, most of Venice and Amsterdam is built on them [pine piles]'.[7] Chips or shavings from deal boards kindled fires. Pine trunks were bored out to provide water pipes for eighteenth-century London, the timber coming from northern Scotland.[8]

An agricultural handbook published in China in the early twentieth century said of the pine tree:

> Its bole can be sawn into planks to make boats or carts . . .
> Branches and needles can be used for fuel . . . its bark and seeds
> can be used for medicine . . . Branches which are not suitable
> for firewood but which contain resin can be used as torches,
> and small trees can be put in a kiln to extract the smoke and
> to make charcoal. Branches which give exceptionally clean
> and delicate soot can be used to make ink.[9]

In 1914, George Russell Shaw observed of the Himalayan species chir pine that

> The wood is used for construction and for the manufacture
> of charcoal, the thick soft bark is valuable for tanning, the

Pine toys.

Early 20th-century Norwegian *tine*, a storage box, made from pine.

resin is abundant and of commercial importance, and the
nuts are gathered for food.[10]

Such statements could be echoed again and again around the world
in pre-industrial societies. A word which is not often mentioned is one
that springs most easily to mind in combination with pine in Europe
and North America: furniture.

A few examples from history illustrate the uses of pinewood
over a broad sweep of time. One very early use of pinewood was discovered unexpectedly. In 1966, archaeologists excavating the site
destined to become the main car park for Stonehenge found a row
of three pits that had evidently held large posts. Traces of wood
from them proved to be pine, which was radiocarbon dated to around
8500–7650 BC (a fourth hole, slightly off the alignment, was found
later). The wood dated from a time when southern Britain was
covered with pine trees, as the climate warmed and vegetation spread
in the wake of retreating glaciers. No one will ever be able to say if
it was chosen for being pine, or simply because it came from large
trees, and the purpose of the posts remains mysterious, though
archaeologists think they probably formed part of a ceremonial or
religious shrine.[11]

From early times, pinewood was used for construction. In about
800 BC, a royal tomb was built in the Phrygian capital of Gordum,
southwest of Ankara in Turkey. Twentieth-century archaeologists
found it to be constructed of various woods, including walls and
cross-beams made from pine, a pattern generally repeated in building remains found in the city. The wood was Scots pine and Austrian
pine, suggesting that substantial pine forests once grew in an area
now largely devoid of trees.[12]

In classical times, Theophrastus said that pine was used for carpentry in houses, and purchases of pinewood are recorded in the
accounts for the Parthenon.[13] In Rome, one factor that was important
in the choice of pinewood was the height of the trees used, as both
masts and an apparent Roman preference for single-span roofs

demanded long timbers. Seneca and Juvenal both commented on timber carts carrying long fir and pine logs, nodding dangerously, and making the streets of Rome shake.[14]

The medieval people of Norway have left a legacy of wooden-built stave churches, mostly made from pine. These buildings, which are 500–700 years old, are made of timbers placed vertically in the ground, in the way in which a palisade is constructed, rather than by the more usual method of placing one plank or log on top of another. Many are elaborate, consisting of several stories placed one on top of another, with the outline broken by steeply pitched roofs and decorated with elaborate carving. They are pine buildings preserved with pine tar: centuries of treating the wood with pitch have given the exteriors of these remarkable buildings a dark red or almost black colour.

John Evelyn reported that the inhabitants of the Canary Islands 'near Tenariff . . . do usually build their houses with the timber of the pitch-trees', but that this was dangerous because of the risk of fire; 'Whenever a house is attacqu'd they make all imaginable hast out of the conflagration and almost despair of extinguishing it.'[15] Fire in wooden buildings, especially those of pine, must have been a constant hazard.

In 1856, Andrew Jackson Downing, the author of *A Treatise on the Theory and Practice of Landscape Gardening Adapted to North America* remarked:

> In the United States, full four-fifths of all the houses built are constructed of the White and Yellow Pine, chiefly of the former. Soft, easily worked, light and fine in texture, it is almost universally employed in carpentry, and for all the purposes of civil architecture.[16]

If the majority of settlers from Europe lived in log cabins or clapboard houses built of pinewood, this was not just because it was easy to use and a good building material, but also because it was close to hand.

Practices recorded among native North Americans illustrate the use of pine for shelter in mobile tribal societies. The tallness and relative lightness of lodgepole pines contributed to their common name:

It was due to these . . . that they were named Lodgepole Pines by Lewis and Clark. Indians of the Great Plains journeyed to the Rocky Mountains to obtain such slender poles for their lodges or tepees.[17]

Another well-recorded use was for tree bark, including that of gray pine and western yellow pine. It was used in conical dwellings built of bark slabs leaning against each other on overlapping layers three or four thick, with pine needles spread on the floor to sleep on.[18] Ponderosa pine roots and gray pine twigs were worked into baskets by native peoples in the American southwest,[19] and the art of making pine-needle baskets appears to be undergoing a revival as a contemporary craft.

From early times, shipbuilding was foremost among the uses for the durable and robust timber of pine. Theophrastus said that it was used for merchant ships (fighting ships were built of fir, which weighs less), and John Evelyn quoted the *Georgics'* 'useful pine for ships', saying:

the true pine was ever highly commended by the Ancients for naval architecture, as not so easily decaying [as the fir]; and we read that Trajan caused vessels to be built out of the true and the spurious kind, well pitch'd and over laid with lead.[20]

But classical references have to be treated with caution, as poets ignored fine distinctions and chose 'pine' or 'fir' depending on how they felt the words suited the narrative or metre. *Pinus* seems to have been a poetic expression for ships generally and could even be extended to mean masts, as in Lucan's 'while the lofty pine is raised', or even to oars. Pine provided planks for the sides of ships and, more importantly, tall, straight trunks for masts. That pine was used for European ships from ancient times into the era of recorded history is borne out by archaeological evidence such as finds preserved in the Viking Ship Museum in Roskilde.

Bulk timber, including pine, was important in northern European trade by the time the Hanseatic League developed sometime in the twelfth century. Trees felled in the Baltic region were sawn up and shipped to North Sea ports, pine timber being carried in pine ships. The pine woods of Scandinavia and Eastern Europe must have seemed limitless, giving the *easterlings*, as the Baltic merchants were called, economic power much resented in England, which had exhausted its native forests by the end of the Middle Ages. The expansion of shipping, for both war and trade, and the need for wood from growing industries, increased demand for pine timber in early modern Europe. Pine, while sought after for specific purposes, was one wood among many; but the European discovery of

Karl Bodmer, 'Sioux Tipi', illustration for Maximilian zu Wied-Neuwied's *Maximilian Prince of Wied's Travels in the interior of North America* (1843–4).

opposite: Detail of Norwegian stave church built of pine timber and preserved with coatings of pine tar.

North America, with its wealth of *Pinus* species growing as magnificent trees in largely undisturbed forests, led to a huge expansion in the use of the wood, and it became a political and economic bargaining point.

Britain, like other European nations, needed pine for ships. In the seventeenth century this was procured at great expense from the Baltic, to Evelyn's dismay:

> What an incredible mass of ready money, is yearly exported into the northern countries for this sole commodity which might all be saved were we industrious at home, or could have more of them out of Virginia.[21]

This demand was particularly influential as the British Navy expanded during the eighteenth century. Pine timber and pine products, such as pitch and tar, were vital and trade was affected by politics. The size and quality of trees, especially eastern white pine in New England, had been noted by the English authorities, which made attempts to reserve

Ivan Shishkin, *Ship Timber*, 1887, oil on canvas. The pine woods of both Eurasia and North America were vital for ship building as late as the end of the 19th century. Russian ones were a favourite subject of Shishkin, who painted them in numerous images.

Charles Warren Eaton, *The Night*, 1911, oil on canvas. The tonalist painter Charles Warren Eaton became known as 'the pine tree painter' because he returned to them as a subject again and again, especially the tall eastern white pines.

particularly fine ones by marking them with the 'broad arrow' indicating government property. This tree, 'remarkably white when newly sawn into planks; whence the common name' and 'more employed in America than any other pine, used for masts',[22] was something they had come to rely on. Eighteenth-century timber duties in Britain gave preference to home and colonially produced wood. In the late eighteenth century, the French made use of supplies of high-quality, easily worked Corsican pine, at that time known as *P. laricio*:

> Previous to the year 1778, the wood was only used by the French government for the beams, the flooring, and the side planks of ships; but in that year the administration sent two engineers to examine the forests of Lonca and Rospa in Corsica, in which abundance of trees were found fit for masts. After this, entire vessels were built with it.[23]

Alexandre Calame, *An Ancient Pine Forest with a Mountain Stream*, 1847, sepia and charcoal with gouache on paper.

This was during the American War of Independence (1775–83), a time when the British Navy found its supplies of eastern white pine from New England cut off. Having failed to stockpile timber of the right quality for repairing masts and spars, the British found themselves forced back to the Baltic for timber during the Napoleonic wars, even though the price was driven up 300 per cent in two years.[24]

This period of high duty on foreign timber briefly allowed exploitation of native pine woods in Britain in the early nineteenth century. Elizabeth Grant of Rothiemurchus on Speyside, Scotland, recorded this in her memoirs of the years 1797–1830. She was fascinated by the forest (which she invariably referred to as firs), and described how the lochs were dammed, ready to provide a head of water for floating logs at

> the proper time for sending them down the streams. It was a busy scene all through the forest, so many rough little horses moving about in every direction, each dragging its

load, attended by an active boy as guide ... This driving lasted
till sufficient timber was collected.[25]

At first, boards were cut in small sawmills close to where trees were
felled, but later logs were floated down the River Spey to larger new
ones. Estate workmen manoeuvred single logs down streams to the
river, where the 'Spey floaters', from families who traditionally worked
in this trade, took charge of them.

Grant left a vivid description of these men,

> to whom the wild river, all its holes and shoals and rocks
> and shiftings, were as well known as had its bed been dry.
> They came up in the season, at the first hint of a spate ... A
> large bothy was built for them at the mouth of the Druie in
> a fashion that suited themselves; a fire on a stone hearth in
> the middle of the floor, a hole in the very centre of the roof
> just over it where some of the smoke got out, heather spread
> on the ground, no window, and there, after their hard day's
> work, they lay down for the night, in their wet clothes – for
> they had been perhaps hours in the river – each man's feet to
> the fire, each man's plaid round his chest, a circle of wearied
> bodies half stupefied by whisky, enveloped in a cloud of steam
> and smoke, and sleeping soundly till the morning.

Floating the logs had its moments:

> There were many laughable accidents during the merry
> hours of the floating; clips would sometimes fail to hit the
> mark, when the overbalanced clipper would fall headlong
> into the water. A slippery log escaping would cause a tumble,
> shouts of laughter always greeting the dripping victims, who
> good-humouredly joined in the mirth. As for the wetting, it
> seemed in no way to incommode them; they were really like
> water-rats.[26]

Log rafts on the Peter the Great Canal near St Petersburg, Russia, 1909, glass plate photograph.

After the Napoleonic Wars, timber lost its profitability for Scottish producers. Today, Rothiemurchus includes areas as close to unspoiled native woodland as one can get in Britain. This quiet, open woodland contains trees of all ages, from saplings to ancient 'granny pines' with bleached dying branches bare of cover against the vivid bark of still-living, mature trees. The lighter foliage and white bark of birches provides a contrast to the massed dark pines. Juniper, bilberry and crowberry form the understorey over lichens and mosses, among which ants, which make mound-like nests from the fallen pine needles, flourish, together with deer, wildcats, red squirrels, capercaillie and crossbills.

Logging and log driving, common practices in the forests of northern Europe, developed on an enormous scale on the west side of the Atlantic when British duty on foreign timber fell after the Battle of Waterloo. Eastern North America offered huge forests containing many commercially valuable species. Supplies of red pine grew conveniently near major rivers in eastern Canada. As in Rothiemurchus, rivers were used for transporting timber. Between 1810 and 1850, most of the accessible timber had been harvested from the river systems of the Miramichi, St John and Ottawa rivers.[27]

Logging in North America commenced with the first snowfall, although there was much autumn preparation – clearing roads for moving timber, moving provisions and building camps with shanties known as cambooses. These, a bigger version of the Strathspey bothies, housed numbers of lumberjacks in a large communal area heated with a central stove. When the snow began to thaw, the timber drive began. Individual logs floated down small rivers into open water, where they were made into rafts. Raftmen built cabins on them and travelled downriver to centres such as Quebec and St John, where vast numbers were held by floating booms adjacent to the sawmills. Log driving continued even after the railways arrived, as it was more economical than transport by rail.

The trade of floating logs was brutal and dangerous, with the ever-present possibility of falling into freezing water or being crushed. Photographs show the extent of the drives. Films survive to show the speed and skill with which the log drivers worked, stepping nimbly along logs which were 'birling', semi-submerged in ice-cold melt-water, both rotating and moving with the current around bends and through rapids, and disentangling the logs from obstructions with long poles armed with hooks on the ends. They have been commemorated in several folk songs. The traditional verses of 'Grand Voyageur sur la Drave' tell of three brothers engaged in the trade, and the prospect of descending the river, including the rapids, far from help if an accident took place. 'River Driver', a traditional Newfoundland folk song, is about life on the river, and the twentieth-century song 'The Log Driver's Waltz', composed by Canadian musician Wade Hemsworth (1916–2002), tells how the agility and lightness of step acquired by log drivers made them sought-after partners on the dance floor. It was used as the theme for a charming short animated film that was much shown on Canadian television in the 1970s and '80s.

Due to the demand for timber, between the Napoleonic Wars and the First World War much of eastern North America was comprehensively logged. Naturalist Edward W. Nelson (1855–1934) recalled the Adirondacks during the American Civil War as being a

> beautiful forest of mixed hardwoods and conifers among which the majestic white pines in all their glory were predominant. Since those days the lumberman's axe has swept those beautiful conifers almost clean.[28]

The pine forests of the eastern USA were, quite simply, too useful.

Apart from their eighteenth- and early nineteenth-century exploitation for shipbuilding, pines had long been sought after for building and many other purposes. Stephen Elliot remarked of eastern white pine that 'From its size and lightness it is preferred for the masts of vessels to all other wood', but also it was

Lumber docks, Jacksonville, Florida, early 1900s.

very extensively used; it is soft, fine grained and light, and free from turpentine; it is therefore used for all the interior work of houses except the floors, and in the Northern States for the covering, and even for the frames.[29]

Longleaf pine, a major source of tar and turpentine, produces a heavy, robust wood which is hard to work and was

more extensively used than any other species of timber we possess. For the frames, the covering, and even the roofing of houses, it is used wherever cypress cannot be obtained; for the flooring of houses, it is preferred to any wood that is known. It is extensively used in ship-building, for the beams, plank, and running timber of vessels. It is used to make the casks in which we ship our rice, and the fencing of our plantations.[30]

In 1914, George Russell Shaw commented that loblolly pine was 'an important tree manufactured into all descriptions of scantlings, boarding'.[31] Shortleaf pine was 'extensively manufactured into material of all kinds that enters into the construction of buildings'.[32] The ubiquity of pine gave North American English several slang expressions, including 'to ride the pine' (in team sports, to sit on the substitutes' bench) and 'pine overcoat' for a coffin.

Iron and steel ships and construction materials reduced the necessity for timber, but the need for fuel wood and charcoal for industrial purposes increased. Ronald M. Lanner detailed the effects this had on a single species and a small area in the American south-west. Here, the pinyon pines of Nevada do not provide good timber – their wood is knotty and their stature generally moderate – but they were conveniently to hand when a silver-mining rush began in 1859. They were used for fuel wood, for shoring mines, for housing and especially for charcoal for smelting. This was so important that skilled Swiss and Italian labour was imported to produce a supply. The brick kilns these people built still stand, and the demand for fuel for one settlement, Eureka, has been estimated at 20 ha worth of pinyon woodland per day alone in the 1870s (as well as another 8 ha worth for domestic use). By 1878, the landscape within 80 km of the town was completely denuded of woodland, taking the deforested area into the orbit of other silver-producing towns with an equal demand.[33]

North American forests were treated as if they had no limits, and about 25–30 per cent of each tree was wasted. Railways and steam power made timber extraction, processing and transport easier in the mid-nineteenth century. They brought competition to the pitch and turpentine industries in North Carolina and the southern USA, making lumber viable for 'timber carpetbaggers' from the northeast. In the western USA the waste that accompanied early logging operations was phenomenal, as massive and ancient trees such as sugar pines were cut for the most utilitarian of purposes:

> much of this valuable resource was squandered from the earliest years of settlement in the Sierra Nevada foothills, the large volume and ease of cutting and working made sugar pine the preferred lumber tree.[34]

It was used for all the requirements of the sudden influx caused by the gold rush – sluice boxes, bridges, houses, barns, fences, pit props, roofing shingles and livestock fences. Some of it went for other purposes, including novelties such as the Wanamaker Grand Court Organ in Philadelphia, constructed in 1904 for the St Louis World's Fair. Sometimes over half a tree would be left to rot. Such practices eventually led to both the development of forestry plantations and the establishment of North American national parks.

As wood for furniture, pine is more useful than ornamental, and as ever it would be used if it was to hand. The qualities of the wood vary between species and places of origin; much pine of northern European and North American origin is whitish-yellow or pinkish-red, although 'pitch pine' is yellower. Scots pine is relatively close-grained, and North American species imported to Europe in the

Udo J. Keppler, 'Who'll Stand by Him?', 1909, an illustration for the magazine *Puck*. Using a forest fire as a visual metaphor for the uncontrolled exploitation of North American forests by timber companies, it shows Gifford Pinchot, chief of the U.S. Forest Service, fighting alone against the flames.

nineteenth century tended to have a coarser grain,[35] perhaps accounting for the splintery nature of Victorian pine floorboards found in many nineteenth-century British houses.

In Britain, with little native pine forest, the wood had to be imported, which made it more expensive before the age of steam than the ubiquity of fitted pine kitchens in the late twentieth century

Udo J. Keppler, 'Protection!', illustration for *Puck* magazine, 1909, when tariffs kept the cost of wood imported to the U.S. high at the cost of eliminating native forests.

would suggest. As red deal, it arrived from the Baltic and was used for panelling and built-in cupboards (often painted) from the mid-seventeenth century onwards. Changes in taste away from panelling and falling transport costs led to it being relegated to the servants' quarters, as a utilitarian wood appropriate for kitchen dressers, rough tables and fittings in sculleries and laundries. Nineteenth-century imports of American pine increased the use for simple, inexpensive furniture of all kinds, and as carcass wood for cheap veneered furniture. A fashion for pale wood furniture – either new, or old pieces stripped of paint or lacquer using caustic solutions – developed in Britain in the 1970s, and pine took its place in this, despite the fact that it tends to darken and turn orangey-red when exposed to light. The pendulum of fashion has swung back towards painted furniture again, this time in the style of Scandinavia, the area in which painted pine furniture might be counted as truly native. Pine, as John Evelyn asserted, can be carved, but is not the choicest wood for this purpose, as it is difficult to undercut.

A new era in the use of pinewood began in the mid-nineteenth century. Pulping developed from the 1840s onwards, using wood chips treated with motion, heat and various chemicals to free the cellulose they contain from lignin, for papermaking. Other applications were soon found, notably in fibres such as rayon and viscose, first commercially produced in the 1890s. Softwoods generally produce longer fibres than hardwoods, and pines, as species that grow in many environments, are much used for the purpose. The methods are general for all sorts of trees, although pine tends to produce a pulp with colour that needs bleaching if a pure white product is required.[36]

Pine used in pulping is determined by factors such as what flourishes conveniently close to a pulp factory, grows easily and swiftly, and is resistant to pests and diseases. Pine species that were considered unimportant in the past found new environments and new applications in the age of plantation forestry and industrial wood use. The discovery that Monterey pine grew fast and to exceptional heights in some southern-hemisphere countries resulted in its use as a plantation tree in New Zealand, South Africa and other countries. Virginia pine is now commercially important for pulpwood, despite its poor form – 'a scrubby species of pine, and its wood is said to be of little value', said Stephen Elliott in 1824.[37] Loblolly pine, pitch pine, red pine, longleaf pine, shortleaf pine, lodgepole pine and jack pine are all quoted as pulpwood species. Like all natural products, individual species have

Vast quantities of pinewood went into carpentry, cheap furniture and household fittings: here it is used to make laundry troughs at Beningbrough Hall, North Yorkshire, the grain emphasized by years of use.

Postage stamp, New Zealand, 1969, one of an issue designed to draw attention to the country's main exports. Monterey pine has spread well beyond the original plantations to threaten the native flora of countries such as New Zealand and South Africa.

subtleties, but these appear of small account for pulp manufacture, which essentially requires trees or the otherwise useless offcuts of trees, such as small branches and knotty wood, at one end and produces wood pulp, a globally traded commodity, at the other.

The industrialization of sawmilling also led to new products such as plywood, spawned from the technology of the newly developed rotary cutter in the 1890s.[38] The traditional uses of pinewood in packaging, building and for general use continued alongside, together with new uses in manufactured building materials such as chipboard. In the 1970s wood from Scots pine, Corsican pine and lodgepole pine was listed as being used for making various items such as telegraph poles, railway sleepers, fencing, building timber for joists, rafters and flooring, sheds, pit props, boxes, wood wool, wallboard and paper pulp.[39]

The over-exploitation of pines and trees generally provoked various reactions, from the establishment of forestry as a science in the countries of the world that were industrializing to a nascent ecological movement, especially in North America. European landowners planted trees both for ornament and as timber in the seventeenth century, but it was the political crises of the late eighteenth century that were a turning point in the history of forestry, as supplies were disrupted and demand increased. This time saw experiments with pine plantations in places as far apart as Scotland, where Scots pine was extensively planted, and in the Dutch colony of Indonesia, where experiments were made with planting Sumatran pine (*P. merkusii*).

The apparently inexhaustible forests of North America could not withstand the coming of railways and the profit motive, and had to be replanted with trees as a crop. Foreshadowing twentieth-century forestry practices, clear cutting of trees followed by replanting had become a standard practice in Germany in the 1840s. The method spread to the rest of the world, even though in Germany reversion to a more sympathetic method of forestry management took place in the 1870s.[40] Deliberate management of forests began in Sweden in the early twentieth century and in Britain after the First World War. Plantation forestry began in North America between the world wars.

Forestry introduced *Pinus* species to the southern hemisphere on a large scale. The British began to establish plantations of pine trees in their southern-hemisphere colonies in the late nineteenth

J.E.H. MacDonald, *Tracks and Traffic*, 1912, oil on canvas. Stacks of cut pine and other timber as part of a busy industrial cityscape. The telegraph poles which frame the picture left and right may well also have been pine posts.

century (1875 in Australia, about 1884 in South Africa and the 1890s in New Zealand). This has taken Monterey pine, especially, a tree whose natural range in California is about 6,000 ha, to a growing area far beyond anything that was possible under natural circumstances – more than 4 million ha for southern-hemisphere timber plantations.[41] Here it flourishes and has become an invasive species, sometimes threatening the original native vegetation, especially in South Africa. Caribbean pine is a successful plantation species for more tropical climates in Brazil and other South American countries, Malaysia and parts of Africa. In places, uncontrolled exploitation of pines still continues, as in Haiti and the Dominican Republic, where political anarchy and subsistence agriculture threaten the native forests of Hispaniolan pine. These trees, providers of excellent-quality wood, once supported an export market.[42]

Intensive forestry to feed demand for timber for construction, pulpwood and other purposes has become associated with blocks of conifers of exotic origin, planted for commercial purposes with little consideration for the landscape. Commercial factors – rapid growth, wood free from knots, resistance to pests and forecasts for demand – are of prime importance. As forestry is a long-term enterprise, there is always the chance that economic circumstances will have changed by the time the trees are ready to harvest, or that growth will not be as good as expected. Thus the lodgepole pine originally planted for timber in Scotland just after the Second World War has limited value and is likely to end up as biomass, or possibly rough packaging wood for pallets and the like.

Pine trees are subject to numerous pests and diseases, many of which have spread as part of human activity. For instance, resin extraction in nineteenth-century North Carolina brought a string of pests in its wake: ips beetles and black turpentine beetles, whose larvae feed on the cambium of the trees; the Southern Pine Sawyer, a moth whose larvae eat the sapwood; and turpentine borers, which feed on the weakened trees, all of which have devastating effects.[43] Forestry plantations unintentionally created ideal conditions for some insect

L.H. Joutel, 'Insects affecting White Pine', illustration from the *Seventh Report of the Forest, Fish & Game Commission of the State of New York* (1902).

pests, such as the pine looper moth (*Bupalis piniaria*), which attacked UK pinewoods in the 1950s, and pine bast scale (*Matsucoccus feytaudi*), which almost eradicated maritime pine plantations in southern Europe during the 1960s. Perhaps the worst example of a problem unintentionally spread by human activities happened in 1910, when a shipment of

eastern white pine reached North America from France. It was carrying a fungal species (*Cronartium ríbicola*, harboured by plants of the *Ribes*
genus such as redcurrants), which proceeded to spread through the white
pines of the continent as white pine blister rust, killing numerous
trees, including the magnificent sugar pines that had already been
devastated by logging activities. Attempts to control the disease through
genetic resistance have led to intensive studies of the affected species.[44]

The industrial use of pine trees (as opposed to softwoods generally) is difficult to elucidate. Statistics tend to be broken down into
hardwoods and softwoods, or by other factors such as ownership and
trunk size. The timber trade recognizes 'red wood' (which strictly
indicates the wood of Scots pine) and 'white wood' (Norway spruce).
Pinewood in the UK is widely used for construction, house building,
joinery and packaging. That from Finland and Russia was – and still is
– favoured, because the northerly environment produces quite slow-
growing trees with relatively strong, stout and generally high-quality
wood.[45] In Britain in the early twenty-first century, conifers account
for just over half the total area of forestry; within this category, the
most important species is actually Sitka spruce (*Picea sitchensis*), accounting for a little over half the area. Scots pine accounts for about another
16 per cent, and lodgepole pine for another 10 per cent.[46]

Pine trees have made a unique contribution to dendrochronology, the science of dating archaeological and historic remains by
tree rings. It originated with observations of Ponderosa pine rings
by astronomer Andrew Ellicott Douglass (1867–1962) in Arizona in
1904. Searching for evidence of the effects of solar phenomena on
plant growth, he evolved a method for counting the rings and marking significant morphological details on individual pieces of wood,
then cross-matching the details. Douglass's method, or developments of it, helped to provide chronologies for both North American
and European tree rings, wood from the genus *Pinus* being a major
contributor to these. In Europe, a chronology for Scots pine 2,012
years long has been established for the post-glacial era, when the
land was too cold for oaks to grow. Many people, however, associate

A cargo of pine timber washed ashore on the coast of Kent, 2009.

dendrochronology with the spectacularly long-lived bristlecone pines of the Colorado Great Basin. These, the oldest living individual plants on Earth, grow in a climate that stresses the tree to its limits, slowing growth and leaving the living branches attached by a slender strip of bark to the roots while the rest of the tree dies. Dr Edmund Schulman studied them in the 1950s; when the oldest living tree was accidentally cut down in 1964, it was discovered to have 4,862 rings.[47] Bristlecone pine rings have helped to provide an exceptionally long chronology for the region in which the trees grow.

Dendrochronology was used to greatest effect by Douglass himself to date the Anasazi ruins of Pueblo Bonito during the 1920s and '30s, when he provided dates for 45 monuments. Forensic

Truck load of ponderosa pine (*P. ponderosa*), Edward Hines Lumber Co. operations in Malheur National Forest, Grant County, Oregon, 1942.

dendrochronology helped convict Bruno Hauptmann, killer of the Lindbergh baby, when a comparison was made between some low-grade pine used in a ladder left at the kidnap scene and floorboards at Hauptmann's home. Patterns left by tools and nails suggested that the pieces matched, and examination of tree-ring patterns confirmed the origin.[48]

The use of pine for timber and pulp may be impressive when it comes to volume, but pinewood and other parts of the tree were – and are – used in many less obvious ways. There are numerous records of pre-industrial and traditional uses of pinewood for its anti-insect and anti-microbial properties. In the tenth century, *Geoponika* mentioned putting splints of resinous pinewood into flour, driving pine stakes in around trees and vines to deter grubs, fumigating hen houses with brimstone, asphalt and pinewood, and cleaning olive oil by dropping burned pine cones into it while they were still hot. Charcoal and soot, by-products of pitch extraction, were used from ancient times for smelting, John Evelyn saying that pine charcoal was 'preffer'd by the Smiths before any other',[49] and that making it and pitch yielded lampblack and printers black for ink.

Lampblack, the sooty residue produced by smouldering pinewood, may seem a fairly minor product, but it was of exceptional importance in China because of the emphasis given to ink here. Records relating to it go back well over 2,000 years. The method for preparing pine soot as described in the seventeenth century AD was careful and complex. If any resin was left in pinewood, the ink would not flow freely, so this was first extracted from the living tree. To do this, a small hole was made at the base and a slow-burning lamp was placed in it. The warmth made the resin gather there and flow out. Then the tree

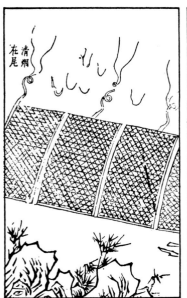

Making Soot for Ink, illustration to the *T'ien Kung Kai Wu* encyclopaedia (1637). The finest and most valued soot came from the end of the structure furthest from the fire, which is being fed with splints of pinewood by a worker.

was felled and cut into pieces, which were burned slowly so that the smoke collected in a specially constructed chamber built of bamboo. This was some 30 m long, and had a channelled brick-and-mud floor and a cover of paper and matting that had holes left in it periodically to allow smoke to escape. After several days the chamber was allowed to cool and the soot was scraped out. The method produced various grades of soot, the best of which was collected furthest from the fire. This was used for the finest ink. Other grades made coarser ink for printing, or pigment for lacquer and plasterers. To make ink, the soot was bound with a water- and protein-based glue, resulting in a malleable substance that was shaped into sticks or blocks whose surfaces provided scope for moulded decoration. Sometimes other substances such as perfumes were added. The best ink was highly valued, much sought after and sometimes literally worth its weight in gold, a subject of art and scholarship, producing a deep, lustrous black with qualities that were much admired and borrowed or imitated by other cultures. Mixed with wine or water and other ingredients, it was also used medicinally.[50]

One of the most visible and ubiquitous uses of pinewood, and possibly the least thought of in the developed world, is in creating light and warmth. Fire runs like a red streak through the human history of pines. This use is difficult for those accustomed to electricity to imagine, but it is still important. Pine banishes the dark, gives warmth and helps start larger fires. The dry, resin-saturated wood splinters and ignites easily.

Pliny the Elder said that pinewood was employed for kindling fires and giving torchlight in religious ceremonies. Torches ran deep in classical mythology and ritual. Demeter carried two flaming torches during her frantic search for her abducted daughter, Kore (Persephone), and the Eleusinian Mysteries of ancient Greece, rooted in the myth of Demeter's search, began with a night-time torch-lit procession. This moved from Athens to Eleusis, about 23 km away, and involved thousands of people; in the otherwise dark landscape the sight must have been extraordinary.[51] Hecate also carried torches. She aided

Pine torches banished the night, and torchlit processions are still impressive.
A modern example: New Year in Shetland.

Demeter's search, but in a painting on an amphora is shown fighting
the giant Klytios, whose hair she has set ablaze with one of them.
Hymen, the god of marriage, carried a torch, and torches were a
feature of Greek and Roman weddings, which took place at night. In
Euripides' play *Trojan Women*, Cassandra, on her way to be 'married'
as a concubine to Agamemnon, uses words that tell vividly of how
their flames appeared:

> Raise the torch and fling the flame! Flood the walls with
> holy light! Worship the Almighty Hymen, God of Marriage!
> . . . I have brought them – torches for my wedding-night,
> leaping light and dancing flame, in your honour, Hymen,
> God of hot desire![52]

In *Medea* a 'torch of frayed pinewood' is mentioned in a wedding
hymn.

Sculptures and frescoes show torches to have been about 1–1½ m
long, slender bundles of splints bound together at intervals along their

Woodcut illustration to Olaus Magnus, *History of the Northern Peoples* (1555). Slips of resinous pinewood were used for inexpensive domestic lighting in many places. This example from Sweden in the mid-16th century shows the inhabitants going about daily tasks carrying lit ones in their mouths and bundles of unlit splints in their belts.

length. Their flames and flickering glow on nights otherwise lit only by the moon and stars were no doubt both impressive and mysterious. They were symbolic of purification as well as giving light. Belief in their power ran deep in the ancient world, and is illustrated in a charm recorded in the tenth century, 'To prevent enchantment of beehives, fields, houses, animal sheds, and workshops', which directed the burial of the hoof of the right foreleg of a donkey under the threshold, along with liquid unburned pine resin, salt and various spices, plus a monthly offering of bread, wool, brimstone and pine torches.[53]

The use of slips of pine for lighting persisted well into the nineteenth century in the Western world. It was recorded in Scotland by Elizabeth Grant: 'the light of a splinter of quick fir Scots pine laid on a small projecting slab within the chimney' lit chilly winter nights in the cottages;[54] and by David Douglas while exploring Oregon in the 1820s. In New England, such slips of pine heartwood became known as candle-wood.

Travellers' tales of the present day tell of the Dali torch festival in Yunnan Province, China, in which participants carry huge torches, throwing what Western backpackers describe as 'powdered resin' at them to produce spectacular sheets of flame, and of pine torches in modern Japan at the Kurama fire festival.

Pine for lighting is ubiquitous in the modern world, although few people give much thought to the origin of the slips of wood found in a box of safety matches. The idea of impregnating slips of pinewood with sulphur to give something that ignited easily and reliably was recorded in China over a thousand years ago. The friction-ignited safety match, the form now common, was developed in Sweden in the mid-nineteenth century.

Pinewood is also excellent firewood. In Mexico in 1909, George Russell Shaw recorded that a vernacular name for both pines and their wood was *ocote* and that bundles of kindling were sold in Mexican city markets under the name. It was

> obtained by slashing the standing tree, and, after allowing time for the resin to accumulate over the wound, by repeating the process at intervals. The chips are tied in small bundles and are retailed in the markets for one centavo each. Trees badly disfigured by the ocote gatherers are frequently seen.[55]

To the chagrin of botanists interested in biodiversity, similar practices have continued to the present day in Mexico, the Middle East, the Himalayas and Southeast Asia.

Bundles of pinewood are still sold as kindling for fires in many countries. This example comes from Turkey.

For those for whom log fires are more linked to aesthetic pleasure, pinewood fires are a fragrant, cheerful, crackling luxury on a chilly night. The botanist Ronald M. Lanner remarks that New Mexicans still make *candelarías*, bonfires with a religious connection inherited from Spanish customs. Backwoods survivalists also make impromptu 'stoves' out of pine logs, sometimes called 'Swedish torches'. About 30 cm in diameter, cloven for most of their length into four, they are lit with a small fire kindled on top and allowed to burn vertically through the wood where the corners of the quarters meet. Once alight, a fire burns down vertically, drawing oxygen through the cuts to keep it going, the top providing a flat surface for heating water or food. The origin of this is variously suggested as backwoods practice in North America, or as something devised by Swedish soldiers during the Thirty Years War (1618–48). The capacity of pinewood to catch fire easily is still useful, and the magic of its light has not been completely extinguished.

five

Pine for Food

ᘉ

As far as food is concerned, pines are best known as a source of edible seeds. Pine nuts, sometimes called pine kernels, are generally harvested by collecting the cones and opening them over heat. Technically, all pine seeds are edible, but most species produce seeds that are simply too small to be of use as human food. Edibility is conferred by size, meaning a seed containing a kernel large enough to be worth collecting and freeing from its shell. Of the twenty or so species whose seeds are used as food, Italian stone pine, cultivated in many parts of the Mediterranean region since ancient times, is an important source. Other Eurasian species that yield nuts are Swiss stone pine, chilgoza pine of the western Himalayas, dwarf Siberian pine and Korean pine. In North America single-leaf pinyon and Colorado pinyon (*P. edulis*) are probably the most important providers, growing from the central and eastern parts of California through Nevada, Utah, Arizona, New Mexico and southwest Colorado. Sugar pine, gray pine, Coulter pine, king pinyon and Mexican pinyon also have edible kernels. Some are of local importance – king pinyon, for example, is a rare tree with a population estimated at 2,500. Its nuts are much prized, but it is harvested in such a destructive manner that its very survival as a species is threatened.[1]

There are subtle variations between pine nuts from different species. They are all about a centimetre long, but vary in shape from a narrow, pointed oval (Italian stone pine), through slim, narrow rods like very large rice grains (chilgoza pine), to slightly triangular, the

139

Pine nuts in their shells: on the right, the slender shape from the Himalayan chilgoza (*P. gerardiana*); on the left, the more triangular shape from the North American single-leaf pinyon, *P. monophylla*.

shape of a sweetcorn kernel (Far Eastern species such as Korean pine) and plump, rounded shapes a little longer than wide, with a slight point at one end (pinyon pine nuts). Pine nuts are off-white to ivory in colour. Those of Italian stone pine are by far the best known to Westerners; they have a crisp texture and a flavour described by Gillian Riley as gentle and slightly resinous, brought out by toasting, gentle frying or baking, but 'their ephemeral aroma can soon turn to rancidity. Nuts with a dark patch at the narrow end are to be avoided.'[2] Fresh pinyon nuts have a moist, tender texture with a slight sweetness in the flavour, and the nuts of Himalayan chilgoza pine are quite oily with a distinct almond note. Pine nuts generally are nutritious, although the proportions of major nutrients (protein, fat and carbohydrate) differ between those from different species. Italian stone pine nuts have a high protein content (34 per cent) and nuts of many species contain anywhere between 40 and 75 per cent fat, although those from single-leaf pinyon have a relatively low fat content of 23 per cent. Carbohydrate content varies widely, from 7 per cent in Italian stone pine nuts to up to 54 per cent in those from single-leaf pinyon.[3]

A footnote to the use of pine nuts as food is a phenomenon called 'pine mouth'. This occurs when someone develops a persistent metallic or bitter taste in their mouth one to two days after eating pine nuts. The sensation can persist for several days to up to two weeks, decreasing the enjoyment of food. It is not, apparently, an allergy, or linked to rancidity in the nuts.[4] Still under investigation by scientists, nuts from Chinese white pine (*P. armandii*), perhaps from varieties of this species that have not hitherto entered the market, are thought to be a likely cause.[5] The demand for pine nuts on world markets is high, and China has become a major supplier.

Pine nuts took their place in Eurasian traditions in a system in which all foods were considered to have specific health benefits, and Pomet remarked that they contained a great deal of oil, were 'pectoral, restorative', and 'sweeten and correct the Acrimony of Humours, increase Urine and Seed, cleanse Ulcers of the Kidneys, resolve, attenuate, and mollify; and may be us'd internally and externally'.[6] He was repeating a very ancient and widespread belief. Apart from their intrinsic qualities of flavour and texture, pine nuts were considered to be aphrodisiac in the ancient Mediterranean world and further east. Galen recommended a mixture of pine seeds, honey and almonds to be taken on three consecutive evenings to increase sexual potency.[7]

The native home of Italian stone pine is unknown because of its long history of cultivation and use, and the earliest history of the use of pine nuts is obscure. Modern European recipes are usually of Mediterranean origin, or at least influenced by Mediterranean habits. Through the long development and transmission of cookery traditions, they have become known throughout Europe, but it is clear that people from countries north of the Alps (many of whom must only have known pine nuts as imports from distant shores) were not, on the whole, as confident with them as those from areas in which the pines grew.

Several recipes that include pine nuts are recorded in the late-Roman compilation of recipes known under the name of *Apicius*. One

Manuscript illumination to the *Taccuinum Sanitatis* (before 1400), showing harvesting of pine cones. Pine nuts were considered warm and dry in the Galenic system of humours; good for the bladder, kidneys and libido.

is for forcemeat faggots, made of chopped meat with fresh white breadcrumbs soaked in wine and seasoned with pepper, fish sauce and myrtle berries. 'You shape the faggots with pine nuts and pepper placed inside. Wrap them in caul fat and roast them.'[8] The habit of putting a few pine nuts in meat mixtures has persisted over the centuries, perhaps reaching its most complex in *Kofta Mabrouma*, a speciality of

Aleppo in Syria, in which a mixture of minced lamb, grated onion and egg is pounded to a pasty consistency, then made into long rolls, each containing a centre of pine nuts; they are formed into circles, each one decreasing in size, and baked in a round tray.[9]

Pine nuts were added to Roman sauces for vegetables and eggs, and to *patina* – like a thick omelette – with numerous other ingredients, including *liquamen* (a salty condiment made from fish) and *defrutum* (made by boiling down grape juice), combinations at once savoury, sweet and a little sour. Such agrodolce mixtures, still including pine nuts, have survived to the present day in Sicilian cookery. In the eastern Mediterranean, a scatter of toasted pine nuts adds texture and flavour to many other dishes, especially rice pilaus and vegetables stuffed with rice or meat mixtures such as *dolmades* (stuffed vine leaves) or aubergines. They provide texture to salads, giving an interesting crunch, and are still added to meatballs not too far removed from the ones detailed by Apicius. They are also scattered over *kibbeh*, a Lebanese dish of raw meat pounded to a paste with bulghur wheat.

Pine nuts add body and flavour to pesto, a classic sauce closely associated with the Italian city of Genoa. For this, garlic, pine nuts, a little salt and a great deal of fresh basil are pounded together using a pestle and mortar to achieve a soft, creamy consistency. The mixture is enriched with grated cheese, either parmesan or pecorino sardo, and thinned with olive oil. Similar sauces have been made since Roman times, using herbs and nuts in various combinations, and the Genoese version was not recorded in print until the late nineteenth century. It is probably the best known example of a pine-nut based food in the twenty-first century. Claudia Roden called it 'the prince of Ligurian dishes' and provided an excellent recipe in her book *The Food of Italy*.[10]

This sauce is so closely identified with northwestern Italy that it is commonly referred to as pesto genovese, and the Genoese claim that only basil grown in the environs of Genoa gives the true flavour. It is mixed with pasta cut in wide ribbons, or eaten as a sauce with other foods. Since the 1980s, outside Italy pesto has become 'fossilised . . . into an industrial product eaten almost exclusively with pasta',[11] and one that does no favours to this delicious sauce. Within Italy, it is actually a much more variable sauce, not always made with pine nuts.

The early European belief that pine nuts, as Pomet said, 'increase seed' (male sexual potency) seems to have led to their incorporation into a number of quasi-medicinal candy recipes. One example, 'Pleasant cordial tablets which are very comforting, and strengthen nature much', was recorded in the mid-seventeenth century by the English nobleman Sir Kenelm Digby:

> Take four ounces of blanched Almonds; of Pine Kernels and of Pistachios, [of each] four Ounces, Eringo-roots, Candid-Limon peels, [of each] three Ounces, Candid Orange peels two Ounces, Candid Citron-peels four Ounces, of powder of white Amber, as much as will lie upon a shilling; and as much of the powder of pearl, 20 grains of Amber-greece, three grains of Musk, a book of leaf gold, Cloves and Mace, of each as much as will lie upon a three pence; cut all these as small as possible you can. Then take a pound of Sugar, and half a pint of water, boil it to a

Pine nuts, basil, garlic, pecorino: some ingredients for *pesto genovese*.

Young Italian stone pines planted along a roadside in the Appenines.

candy-height, then put in the Amber-greece and Musk, with three or four spoonfulls of Orange flower water, Then put in all the other things and stir them well together, and cast them upon plates, and set them to dry; when both sides are dry, take Orange-flower-water and Sugar, and Ice them.[12]

This recipe probably shares a common origin with *penande*, a candied confection of pine nuts with sugar, honey, mace and cloves recorded in a late fifteenth- or early sixteenth-century English manuscript.[13] Such confections represented a widespread European tradition of sweet mixtures, more or less pleasant to eat, which involved ingredients considered to be good for particular health problems, or to be cordial – good for the heart, keeping the body in optimum health. The early belief in pine nuts, almonds and honey as aphrodisiacs probably gave rise to many such sweets. *Pinoccata*, now a speciality of Perugia but once made all over Italy, is a confection of pine nuts and chopped candied peel mixed with sugar syrup spread over wafers, and they are added to *panforte*, a mixture of ground nuts and fruit associated with Siena.

Pine nuts are incorporated into confectionery and other foods all around the Mediterranean. These almond paste balls rolled in pine nuts are of North African origin.

Other confections made with pine nuts include various marzipan-type mixtures of sweet almond paste rolled in or otherwise decorated with pine nuts, linked to the traditions of the Muslim cookery of the Mediterranean coast of North Africa. Pine nuts are added to baklava fillings and scattered over cakes. Sweets made from pine nuts in the manner of sugared almonds, panned with thin, crisp sugar shells, are known both in Italy and Spain.

A much more unusual use of pine nuts was recorded in late seventeenth-century Italian collections: for ice creams. To make *sorbetta di torrone*,

> you need a third [of a *rotolo*, which was around 800g] of Naples pine kernels, half a quarter of almonds, put into fresh water a day before use, and if there is not time, use really hot water so that they swell up quickly, and rub them well with your hands to make them turn white, and then pound them altogether several times, moistening them with some of the water and strain. . . you need three quarters of sugar. Ambergris or musk as flavouring, and you need a tornese of well ground coriander seeds, diluted in half a *giarra* [a jar, a

local measurement of liquid] of water, strained into the said ice when it is grainy; you also need to add two ounces of almonds chopped in four, or two ounces of pine kernel comfits.[14]

Pine nuts are occasionally mentioned in connection with other early-Italian ice-cream recipes, and in the twentieth century Annissa Helou recorded a Lebanese one using pine-nut 'milk' thickened with mastic and salep.[15] She also describes collecting pine cones during holidays in the mountains, and attempting to open them between two stones:

> The secret was how to scale the strength of the hit so that we broke the shell without crushing the nut, a feat which we occasionally achieved. They [pine cones] can also be eaten green. The fresh ripe cone is cut with a knife into wedges and the soft, fleshy pine kernels are taken out, dipped in salt and eaten whole.[16]

Another part of the world where people relished pine nuts is northern India and the Afghanistan region of the Himalayas, where 'One tree, one man's life in winter', a proverb from Kunawar, refers to the seeds of chilgoza pine.[17] The Latin name remembers Captain Alexander Gerard (1792–1839), who mentioned pine nuts several times under different local names, including a 'pine called Ree which bears the Neosa nut'. For him, like many people of British descent, pine nuts seem to have been a novelty and he struggles to describe them, saying that 'in shape and taste it very much resembles the pistachio'.[18] Pine nuts also play a role in the food of the native people of Siberia, where they are pressed for oil.[19] Used uncooked in salad dressings and the like, various health claims are made for pine-nut oil, including that it benefits the digestive system and acts as an appetite suppressant.

In North America, native peoples made extensive use of the nuts of various pine species, probably spreading them along trails by dropping seeds accidentally. Evidence for human use of pine kernels among the early inhabitants of North America starts around 6,000 years ago with charcoal and seed shells from single-leaf pinyon at Gatecliff shelter in central Nevada.[20] Spanish colonists, as inhabitants of the Mediterranean world, were familiar with pine nuts as food. Their name for pine, *piñon*, gave pinyon as a collective term for pines with edible nuts in this area, because Spanish explorers were familiar with Italian stone pines and recognized these trees as similar. The survivors of a Spanish shipwreck in 1528 wandered from the Gulf coast to California, on their way observing that some natives ate pine nuts 'better than those of Castile because they have very thin shells'.[21] Sixteenth-century Spanish expeditions continued to record the use of pine nuts among the natives of the area, and later ones were saved from starvation by gifts or purchases of food, including pine nuts, from local natives.

Settlers of northern European origin, crossing to California from the 1840s onwards, came from areas in which pine trees produced seeds

Jan Davidsz. de Heem's *Still-life with a Tazza and an Ornamented Cup*, 1653, oil on canvas, showing pine nuts in the filling of a rich pie.

too small to be worth eating. They nearly starved when passing through Nevada, apparently unaware that the trees around them carried crops of nutritious seeds. Colonists of northern European origin in the southwestern USA tended to overlook the significance of pine nuts in aboriginal life. 'Very few of our native species are looked upon as having any economic importance in these days of the white man', said Californian botanist Willis Linn Jepson in 1909.[22] Nineteenth-century northern Europeans would have had little experience of pine nuts on their home territory, and therefore lacked the knowledge to investigate American pine trees as sources of food.

In native North American tribal myth, pinyon pine and its nuts are entwined with the notion of origins. The Navajo say it was planted by the squirrel and that the nuts were food for the early peoples, while others believe it to be the oldest of trees and the provider of food to people of the past.[23] Some of the most striking monuments of human occupation in the area, the cliff dwellings of Mesa Verde, are built in pinyon woodland, in part perhaps because of this rich and easily available supply of food, which allowed a surplus of energy for settlement building. Gray pine took a (now-disused) common name, 'digger pine', from the contemptuous term European settlers gave to native tribes in the American southwest. It derived from their habit of digging for edible roots in spring and summer, but applied to pine trees also indicated their use of seeds from its massive cones (gray pine cones can weigh up to 1 kg each).

Records tell how various tribes went to the pinyon woods to collect nuts; in the case of single-leaf pinyon they were in competition with jays, and collected the cones while they were still young and green, opening them using fires.[24] The writer and naturalist John Muir described this harvest in the 1870s among the Paiute tribe, saying how members of the tribe made ready their beating poles and collected bags, baskets and sacks. Those working for white settlers left their employment and gathered with the rest of the tribe, everyone mounted on ponies, then they started out

Alfred Hartley, *Stone Pine in Moonlight*, late 19th or early 20th century, print.

in great glee to the nut-lands, forming curiously picturesque cavalcades; flaming scarfs and calico skirts stream loosely over the knotty ponies, two squaws usually astride of each, with baby midgets bandaged in baskets slung on the backs or balanced on the saddle-bow; while nut-baskets and water-jars project from each side, and the long beating-poles make angles in every direction. . . . the squaws with baskets, the men with poles ascend the ridges to the laden trees, followed by the children. Then the beating begins right merrily, the burrs fly in every direction, rolling down the slopes, lodging here and there against rocks and sage-bushes, cached and gathered by the women and children . . . Smoke-columns speedily mark the joyful scene of their labors as the roasting fires are kindled, and, at night, assembled in gay circles garrulous as jays, they begin the first nut feast of the season.[25]

Muir said of single-leaf pinyon, or nut pine as he called it, that 'A more contentedly fruitful and unaspiring conifer could not be conceived.'[26]

It was 'quite the most important food-tree on the sierra', the nuts being 'sweet to every palate, being eaten by birds, dogs, squirrels, horses and men'.[27]

North American native peoples prepared the nuts in various ways. First they shelled them on a metate (saddle quern), then they could be eaten raw or whole, ground into nut butter and spread on freshly made corncakes, or made into soups or mushes. For some Native Americans they were merely a supplement to other foods, but for others, such as the Great Basin Shoshone, Northern Paiute and Washo, they were staple foods, deeply embedded in their culture.[28] Green cones from gray pines were also used, after being twisted off the trees by hand in the spring. They were beaten with a stone, the covering was peeled off and the nuts, which were soft-shelled at this stage, were eaten shell and all. The pithy centre of the cone was roasted in hot ashes to give a slightly sweet food.[29]

Sugar pine also provided nuts. Jepson recorded how in autumn

> the tribe went on a long journey to the high mountains . . .
> where the Sugar Pines grow on the ridges, and celebrated . . .
> by tree-climbing contests among the men. The large cones of
> the Sugar Pine carry a goodly supply of small but very sweet-
> kerneled seeds.[30]

The nuts were harvested by climbing the very tall trees and swaying the branches until the cones twisted off. The pitch was burned off and the nuts were extracted and winnowed. Sometimes they were pulverized until they had the consistency of peanut butter. This nut butter was made specially for feasts and eaten with acorn soup.[31]

Pine seeds have led botanists to new species at least twice. David Douglas discovered sugar pines when his curiosity was aroused by some exceptionally large pine seeds in a smoking pouch belonging to a local Indian in northern Oregon. More recently, king pinyon was discovered after its seeds were found for sale in a Mexican market.[32]

On a practical note, for those who have managed to obtain un-shelled pine nuts, the shells vary in thickness. Those of chilgoza pine are thin and delicate and can be cracked between the fingers. The shells of nuts from pinyon pines are tougher, and need gentle pressure from something like a rolling pin to crack the shells (but with too much pressure, the kernel smashes and is useless). Cracking them between the teeth is not to be recommended, as the shells are hard. Store pine nuts in a cool place or freeze them (in which state they will keep indefinitely). If you are lucky enough to have fresh pinyon nuts, leave them in their shells and store in paper or cloth bags in a cool place. They will dry out and 'cure' as they age, losing their fresh, soft texture and shrinking. Once cured, they keep well. Many recipes call for pine nuts to be toasted lightly before they are added to dishes, especially when they are to be scattered over rice or salads as garnishes. This enhances their texture and brings out their slightly resinous flavour.

Apart from providing nuts, pine trees are not an obvious source of food, but a few other food uses are recorded. One of the most curious is the 'pine honey' of southwestern Turkey and Greece. As culinary historian Mary Isin explains, this is not honey in the true sense (pine trees do not flower and therefore do not produce nectar), but an insect-derived food, a form of manna: honeydew produced by the scale insect *Marchalina hellenica*.

> Known as balsıra, the honeydew is deposited on the branches of some pine species, particularly the Turkish pine . . . by the immature insects. During the hot summer months the quantity of the saccharine liquid increases and attracts bees, which collect this syrup instead of nectar from flowers. During the balsıra season Turkish beekeepers from far afield transport their hives to the pine forests of the region.[33]

This practice has been known since the seventeenth century, when an account was given of pine honey, how it was gathered by hand and

the remaining honey is left on the trees and the bees of the
province come to those pine-clad mountains and carry it away
to their nests in their hives and make great combs of honey that
are famous in the four corners of the world as Sıgla or Sivrihisar
honey, which has a fragrance like musk and raw ambergris . . .
and from this is made strained honey as white as muslin that
is sent as gifts to magnates and gentry.[34]

Other pine products in Turkey include pine syrup and *çam reçeli*, a
jam made from young pine cones. The use of pine for food and
flavouring by traditional rural communities around the world is far
more extensive than written sources suggest.

Sugar pine takes its common name from the sugary sap (not resin)
that exudes from deep wounds to the tree. Indigenous North Americans
used this before Europeans brought sugar to the Pacific northwest as
a sweetmeat. John Muir said:

The sugar, is to my taste the best of sweets – better than
maple sugar. It exudes . . . in the shape of irregular, crisp,
candy-like kernels . . . Indians are fond of it, but on account
of its laxative properties, only small quantities may be eaten.

This is not sugar in the sense of cane- or beet-derived sucrose, but a
sugar-alcohol called pinitol (monomethyl D-inositol).[35] Resin from
other pine species, such as ponderosa pine and gray pine, was also
chewed like gum.

Apart from these uses, pine trees seem mostly to have provided
starvation or subsistence foods, or to have been used for medicine.
Aylmer Bourke Lambert said:

We are informed by Linnaeus that the Laplanders eat, during
the winter, and sometimes even during the whole year, a

overleaf: The characteristic shapes of Italian stone or umbrella pines, seen here in the
Strophylia Forest in Greece, are part of the Mediterranean landscape.

preparation made of the inner bark of the pine . . . called,
among these people, bark-bread. . . . the dry and scaly external bark is carefully taken off, and the soft, white, fiborous
and succulent matter collected and dried. . . . When the
natives are about to convert it to use, it is slowly baked on
the coals, and being thus rendered more porous and hard is
then ground into powder, which is kneaded with water into
cakes and baked in an oven.[36]

Similar practices were reported among the native peoples of the
eastern USA, especially using eastern white pine, and the American
outdoorsman Euell Gibbons decided to try cooking and eating it. He
boiled some inner bark from white pine 'and it reduced to a glutinous
mass from which the more bothersome wood fibers were easily removed.
. . . palatability left much to be desired'. Following the reported native
practice of cooking the bark with meat, he 'tried boiling some with beef,
but . . . felt that instead of making the bark edible I had merely ruined
a good piece of beef'. Dried, powdered and made into a kind of bread,
he found the bark had a slight turpentine smell and a taste that, while
initially very sweet, was followed by persistent bitterness and astrin-
gency. He also experimented with candying peeled new shoots of
white pine, a practice recorded among New Englanders ('I would
have considered it a pretty good tasting cough medicine . . . but I'm
sure I have eaten much better confections.'). Pine needles are rich in
vitamins A and C. Eventually he concluded that

> Pine Needle Tea, made by pouring 1 pint of boiling water
> over about 1 ounce of fresh white pine needles chopped fine,
> is about the most palatable pine product I have tasted. With a
> squeeze of lemon and a little sugar it is almost enjoyable.[37]

Gibbons was not reliant on gathered foods; people in the past were less
fortunate. In his diary, David Douglas recorded arriving at Spokane
to find that his host there had no food to offer; Mr Finlay and his

family had been living for six weeks on the roots of camas (*Camassia quamash*, a member of the lily family) and

> a species of black lichen which grows on the pines. The manner of preparing it is as follows: it is gathered from the trees and all the small dead twigs taken out of it, and then immersed in water until it becomes perfectly flexible, and afterwards placed on a heap of heated stones with a layer of grass or leaves between it and the stones to prevent its being burned; then covered with the same material and a thin covering of earth and allowed to remain until cooked, which generally takes a night. Then before it cools it is compressed into thin cakes and is fit for use.[38]

Pine woods are a renowned as a rich source of fungi of various species, including the *Polyporus* species, in China considered to be an excellent medicine for those wishing to prolong life.

A charming story tells that the smoky flavour of Lapsang Souchong tea was invented by accident

> when some soldiers camped in a tea factory filled with fresh leaves and processing was delayed. When the soldiers left the workers realised that it was too late to dry the tea leaves in the usual way if they were to get the tea to market in time. So they lit open fires of pine wood to speed up the drying process.[39]

And, recalling an ancient belief in the pine cone as a symbol of fertility, tiny fritters of dough, drenched in honey- and orange-flavoured syrup, called *pignoccata* (entirely unrelated to pine in terms of ingredients but evoking an ancient connection of pine cones with fertility), are made for carnival in Palermo or Christmas in Messina.[40]

six

Mythic Pine, Artist's Pine

H uman thoughts about pine in antiquity seem to have varied widely. There are two strands, both complex, which come from opposite ends of Eurasia. One is Mediterranean, about classical gods and their followers, often involving violent imagery; the other is Chinese, about the tranquil wisdom achieved with old age. Northern Europeans and Siberian shamans also held beliefs about pine trees, often to do with midwinter renewal. Other cultures, especially those of pre-Columbian North America, had symbolic myths about pine trees, but they are less well recorded or have been lost in the onslaught of modernity.

In the ancient Mediterranean world pine was sacred to Zeus,[1] Poseidon and Dionysus. Themes include metamorphosis and purity (the trees and branches, the Pitys myth), fertility (the cones) and bloodthirsty death. Pine wreaths were awarded to victors of the Isthmian Games held in honour of Poseidon. Pan wore a pine wreath,[2] and so did Diana, the virgin huntress. Chloe, too, wore a *pinea corona*, which Daphne took from her and put on her own head.[3]

In classical Greece pine cones were connected with fertility, a belief that may have been of ancient origin. Assyrian reliefs from the ninth and eighth centuries BC show genii, mythical winged men, holding pine-cone-shaped objects (identification is not certain) and apparently fertilizing trees with them. In Greece and Rome, pine-cone fertility symbolism is more obvious. During the ancient festival of Thesmophoria, pine cones and other symbols of fecundity were thrown into the sacred vaults of the goddess Demeter, and cone-tipped wands or staffs, probably phallic symbols, were borne by the followers of Dionysus, god of wine. He had another link with pine trees. The Delphic Oracle had commanded the Corinthians to worship a particular pine tree equally with him, so they made two images of Dionysus out of it, with red faces and gilt bodies.[4]

Darker, bloodier tales associate pine trees with Attis, a vegetation god of the Phrygians (a Bronze Age people of Anatolia) who was beloved of Cybele, mother of the gods, and, in the convoluted way of mythology, perhaps her son, or born of a girl who became pregnant when she took an almond from a tree that in turn had sprung from the genitals of the castrated Agdistis, demon son of Zeus and Cybele. Gods of vegetation often met violent deaths followed by resurrections, and there are two versions of the death of Attis. One tells that, like Adonis, he was killed by a boar; the other that he castrated himself and bled to death under a pine tree (his priests castrated themselves on entering his service).[5] After his death, Attis was changed into a pine tree. His cult became established in Rome, celebrated in March when a pine tree was cut down, brought to the sanctuary of Cybele and treated as a divinity. A special guild of tree-bearers undertook the task. The trunk was treated like a corpse, swathed in woollen bands. Wreaths of violets – flowers that were supposed to have sprung from

Edward Calvert, *Pan and Pitys*, mid-19th century, drawing.

the blood of Attis – decorated it, and an effigy of the god was attached to the tree.

Frazer, recounting the myth of Attis in *The Golden Bough*, remarked that it had a savagery 'that speaks strongly for its antiquity'.[6] He speculated that for the Phrygians, the evergreen nature of pine in fading autumn woods 'may have seemed to their eyes to mark it out as the seat of a diviner life . . . exempt from the sad vicissitudes of the seasons, constant and eternal as the sky which stooped to meet it.'[7]

Another reason for the sanctity of the pine, he suggests, may have been related to pine nuts. The rites of Cybele were orgiastic, and perhaps connected to wine brewed from pine nuts.[8] A further dark and bloody myth told of Marsyas, a satyr or herdsman and a friend of Cybele, who challenged Apollo to a musical contest. Vanquished and tied to a pine tree, he was flayed by the god, Frazer suggesting this may once have been the fate of the priest of Cybele himself.[9]

Pine cones have fascinated humans for millennia. Leonardo of Pisa, also known as Fibonacci, described in 1202 the ratio by which the size of the scales increases: the Fibonacci sequence of 1, 1, 2, 3, 5, 8 . . . , common in nature. But long before this, their most consistent and visible manifestation in the art of the classical Mediterranean world was in the iconography of Dionysus (Bacchus), god of wine: Dionysus who bounds though the pine forests of Parnassus with thyrsus and deer skin.[10]

The thyrsus was a long staff (sometimes said to be a stem of wild fennel), tipped with a pine cone and borne by Dionysus and his followers, the maenads or bacchantes, the 'raving ones'. It is interpreted as a phallic fertility symbol, and is common in representations of Dionysus and his initiates. In the Villa of the Mysteries in Pompeii there are murals depicting initiation rites undertaken by women entering the cult. One shows the god sprawling on the steps of a throne at the feet of his mother, Semele, or possibly his consort, Ariadne, whose arms support him, his ribbon-decorated, pine cone-tipped staff running diagonally across the fresco. Other paintings show a series of frightening and painful initiation rites, after which

Baldassare Peruzzi, *Cybele in a Chariot drawn by Lions*, 1496 – 1536, pen and brown ink with brown wash. Detail of print showing Cybele holding a pine cone and ears of wheat, symbols of fertility.

the cowering initiate is presented with a thyrsus of her own.[11] There are numerous other representations, especially on Greek black- or red-figure ceramics. Dionysus riding a leopard, cone-tipped thyrsus in hand with ribbons flying, appears on a fourth-century BC mosaic from Pella, capital of ancient Macedonia. Classical sculptures also carry numerous representations of the thyrsus, Dionysus, the maenads and other followers such as Silenus.

Fresco depicting initiation into the cult of Bacchus, second half of first century BC, from the Villa of the Mysteries, Pompeii. A new initiate cowers over the knees of a nurse while another woman presents her with a pine-cone-tipped thyrsus.

The maenad was popular with European artists from the seventeenth century onwards, appealing strongly to 'Victorians in Togas', a number of nineteenth-century neo-Classical painters who used it as a pretext for depicting beautiful young women in various stages of abandonment, very different from the received conventions of femininity of the time. John William Godward (1861–1922) painted the image of a priestess of Bacchus carrying a thyrsus at least four times. John Maler Collier (1850–1934)'s *Priestess of Bacchus* wears the maenad's animal skin and an ivy wreath and carries a cone-tipped thyrsus, but has the expression of one about to bring the maenads to order. William-Adolphe Bouguereau (1825–1905), a French academic painter, also took bacchantes as subjects, favouring semi-draped nudes that veered towards the pornographic. In *Faun and Bacchante* the maenad is supported by a grinning faun, her limbs heavy with wine and a thyrsus prominent along the lower edge of the painting. Bouguereau's *Bacchante on a Panther*, decorating a plate, echoes the Pelle mosaic, but the rider is a semi-naked girl, feet decorously crossed, brandishing her thyrsus.

Mediterranean antiquity produced many votive stone pine cones – several found on Cyprus date from 1000 BC to the third to first century BC. Pine-cone forms also appear on Roman glass jugs and flasks dating from the first and second centuries AD. An enormous bronze pine cone was cast as a fountain in the first or second century AD by Publius Cincius Salvius Libertus and placed in the Campus Martius area of Rome, where it gave the name to the IX rione (district), Rione della Pignia. It was moved to the Vatican by Pope Symmachus, and into a specially designed niche in the Cortile del Belvedere in the seventeenth century.[12] Dante referred to it in the *Divine Comedy* as the pine cone of St Peter in Rome.

In the applied arts during the eighteenth and nineteenth centuries, pine cones became simple decorative motifs, as in the Royal Worcester pine-cone pattern introduced for decorating the company's china in about 1770. Other famous companies that used the motif included Tiffany's, who employed it on a silver bowl, and Fabergé, for which it provided inspiration for both a jewelled egg and a pine-cone decanter stopper. Pine cones were also fashionable motifs in eighteenth- and nineteenth-century silverwork as knobs for teapot lids.

Every age reinterprets the past through its own vision, and for twenty-first century viewers the idea of the pine-cone symbol seems less associated with phallic fertility and more with the notion of mystic wisdom, if Internet searches are anything to judge by. This is principally because of interest in the pineal gland, the small organ

Bronze fountain in the form of a pine cone, first century AD, now located in a courtyard of the Vatican.

shaped like a pine cone, deep in the brain, which has come to be associated with the idea of the 'third eye' in eastern mysticism.

Pine trees and pine boughs are less frequent motifs, perhaps because they were more difficult to depict. A mosaic from Pompeii shows Pitys turning into a pine tree. The mid-sixteenth-century Fountain of Neptune by Bartolomeo Ammannati in Piazza della Signoria in Florence shows the god with an iron crown of pine needles and cones, echoing the pine wreath at the ancient Isthmian Games.

With their foliage magically persisting through the dark and cold of the northern winter, evergreen trees of all sorts have long intrigued Europeans. Festivals in Scandinavia and northern Russia celebrated spring resurrection and new growth in June into recent times.[13] Supernatural powers were still attributed to pines in late sixteenth-century Livonia, according to the anonymous author of *Cultus Arborum*, who recounts that Leonard Rubenus, a monk passing through Estonia,

> saw there a pine tree of extraordinary height and size, the branches whereof were full of divers pieces of old cloth and its roots were covered with many bundles of straw and hay. He asked a man of the neighbourhood what was the meaning of it; he answered that the inhabitants adored that tree, and that the women after a safe delivery brought thither these bundles of hay; that they also had a custom to offer at a certain time a tun of beer.[14]

Rubenus, however, cut a cross in it, then a gibbet, as a sign of contempt.

Other accounts in *Cultus Arborum* mention how branches from *Frau Fichte* ('Mrs Spruce'), the pine of Silesia, were decorated with coloured paper and spangles, carried about by children on mid-Lent Sunday, and suspended above the doors of stables in the belief that they would prevent harm to the animals. Another belief included the idea that the pine was inhabited by wind spirits 'owing to the whispering noise proceeding from it in the breeze', the holes and knots being the means of ingress and egress, and a beautiful woman of Småland, really an elf, left her family through a knot-hole in the wooden wall. In parts of Germany, one way to cure gout was for a patient to climb a pine tree and tie a knot in the topmost shoot, saying as he did it, 'Pine, I bind here the gout that plagues me.'[15]

Further east, the Buryats, a tribal people living around Lake Baikal, revered groves of trees, including those of Scots pine. They were shaman forests, to be ridden through in silence for fear of offending the spirits of the woods. Here too, solitary trees near villages were adorned with talismans, ribbons and sheepskins. They were called pines, even if, in practice, they were larches. Buryat shrines can still be found, constructed of poles and adorned with fabric strips and small offerings, in places as directed by the shaman.[16]

On the shores of Lake Baikal, a pine 'shaman tree' wrapped and tied with strips of cloth.

Ethnographers and folklorists have long noted an association between evergreens – pines, firs, holly, ivy – and midwinter festivals, ascribing this to the living greenery of the trees at a point when so many other plants seem dead. The Christmas tree, famously said to have been transplanted from Germany to Britain by Prince Albert, must be an echo of this, but its sentimentalized and domesticated form has lost any echoes of paganism. Hans Christian Andersen published a cautionary tale known in English as *The Little Pine Tree* (or sometimes, *The Little Fir Tree*), about a conifer wishing that it could grow up and become a beautifully decorated Christmas tree, with little thought as to what happened to a discarded tree. Pines compete with firs and spruces in the specialist market for twenty-first century Christmas trees, sensitive to factors such as price and 'needle drop'. In twentieth-century Russia, the custom of the *yëlka*, Christmas tree, migrated to New Year and was celebrated as enthusiastically as politics allowed. In post-glasnost Vladivostok, American writer Sharon Hudgins noted the trees waiting to be taken into apartments of high-rise flats, 'suspended upside down from window ledges to keep them cold and fresh, looking like uprooted evergreens blown there by the wind'.[17]

Pines are uncommon in the art of medieval and early modern Europe. They occur in illuminated manuscripts recounting *Le Roman de la Rose*, where a garden contains a 'fountain 'neath a glorious pine, a pine so tall, straight-grown and fair'.[18] Sandro Botticelli painted four panels depicting the story of Nastagio degli Onesti. This recounts a tragedy doomed ever to repeat itself in ghostly form, as a knight hunts to death the maiden who has spurned him in the pine forest of Ravenna. Botticelli's paintings suggest how a pine forest looked in the fifteenth century, with a clear forest floor, the slender upright trunks of the trees making a visually rhythmic pattern as they recede into the distance, each topped by a dark, spreading crown. This shape was produced partly by lopping trees for fuel wood. Botticelli depicts two woodcutters in fetching and distinctive clothing – red tights, grey tunics and black hats attached to bands to prevent them from blowing away. He also includes images of rabbits and deer that suggest animals for hunting.

Pine-tree images became more frequent in the nineteenth century, when (in the generalized sense of conifers) they featured in the paintings of landscape painters, and later in the work of the Impressionists. Caspar David Friedrich (1774–1840), a German Romantic

Sandro Botticelli, *The Story of Nastagio degli Onesti* (first episode), *c.* 1483, tempera on panel. The ghostly hunt takes place in the Ravenna *pineta*, a forest of umbrella pines originally planted in the early middle ages.

painter, executed many images of pine trees against dramatic lighting conditions. *Cross on the Mountain* (1808), one of several paintings the artist made of this subject, depicts a cross against pine or fir trees, in turn silhouetted against a golden sunset sky, their spires echoed by a church in the background. *Morning* (*c.* 1820), showing the mist rising from a conifer forest against a dawn sky, is a less dramatic setting for pine trees, but one that still evokes feelings of spirituality associated with trees in vast landscapes, and a theme also much used by painters in Chinese and Japanese traditions. Pine trees recur in some of Friedrich's other works – in snow, as backdrops for hunting or for waterfalls, and as trees enclosing smaller and more intimate, but still natural spaces.

The spiritual, deep quiet of pine forests was evoked later in the nineteenth century and during the early twentieth century by Russian landscape painters. Ivan Shishkin (1832–1898) became famous for images of pine forests, one of his best-known works being *Morning in a Pine Forest* (1889, reproduced on p. 46), in which a group of bears plays on fallen trunks in a primeval pine forest. Shishkin, too, referred to the subject of pine trees in all moods and weathers – summer sun and winter snow, and as settings to walk through or in which to contemplate flowing water.

Northern conifer forests were also a subject for Finnish painters from the early nineteenth century onwards. Pekka Halonen (1865–1933) reflected this tradition, painting both the natural aspects of pines, particularly as they appear shrouded in heavy winter snow, their straight branches bowed and softened under masses of white (for instance *Winter Landscape at Kinahmi*, 1923), and the human one of clearing forest to use the land for agriculture (*Pioneers in Karelia*, 1900).

The Impressionists and their followers observed landscapes in a very different climate, producing images full of sunlight and Mediterranean colour. Paul Cézanne (1839–1906) painted *The Large Pine* at least twice (in 1889 and 1895–7). Vincent van Gogh (1853–1890) left images of *Pine Trees with Dandelions* (1890), his eye caught by the textural rhythms of pine bark and the manner in which the light on

Caspar David Friedrich, *Winter Landscape with a Church*, c. 1811, oil on canvas.

it was echoed by dandelion clocks, and *Pine Trees Against Setting Sun with Red Sky* (1889). The dark, compact shapes of umbrella pines as a feature of the French Riviera appear in the work of pointillist Paul Signac (1863–1935), their foliage massed against vibrant coastal light in *Umbrella Pines at Caroubiers* (1898) and *The Pine Tree at St Tropez* (1909).

Pine trees captured the attention of The Group of Seven, Canadian painters who, working at the turn of the nineteenth and twentieth centuries, produced striking and enduring images with influences from Impressionism, Japanese art and Expressionism. Painting from nature in summer and working up canvases in the studio in winter, their work includes some well-known depictions, especially *The Jack Pine* (Tom Thomson, 1916–17, reproduced on p. 186), a single tree silhouetted against a sky of cold pale greens and golds, distant snow-flecked purple mountains and a lake that reflects the sky. Although 'Western' in materials, techniques and concept, the composition is reminiscent of Japanese *haramatsu* (pines by the seashore) scenes. A single pine tree or group of pines with water, mountains and sky recurred in the Canadian painters' work as, among others, *The West*

Paul Signac, *Sails and Pines*, 1896, oil on canvas. Signac's pine trees, like those in some Japanese prints, create an intense contrast in the landscape.

Wind (Tom Thomson, 1916–17); *Stormy Weather, Georgian Bay* (F. H. Varley, c. 1920); *Night, Pine Island* (A. Y. Jackson, 1924); and *Evening Silhouette* (Arthur Lismer, 1928). More prosaic aspects of the Canadian forest are represented: *The Fire Ranger* (Franz Johnston, 1921) shows the vastness of the Canadian landscape, a huge summer sky of cotton-wool clouds receding above irregular, forest-covered hills, and the fire ranger himself indicated by the small detail of a biplane dwarfed by forest and sky. *Summer Day* (Tom Thomson, *c.* 1915) shows an even larger expanse of sky, the land a distant shore across a lake scattered with a few isolated, apparently dead trees remaining from a clear-cut or fire. *Tracks and Traffic* (J.E.H. MacDonald, 1912) shows the implications of all this for the Canadian economy: stacked, sawn timber in the snow against a steam train, and an industrial landscape of gas holders and mill chimneys.

Botanical illustrations provided an alternative way of depicting pine trees in Western art, for the eye isolates details in a way that is impossible for the camera to achieve. A necessity for science before the development of photography, they still show details of plants more clearly than any photograph. Those by Ferdinand Bauer in Alymer Bourke Lambert's *The Genus Pinus* are some of the most beautiful illustrations of pines of all time. Drawings in other books, such as those in George Russell Shaw's *Genus Pinus*, while both excellent and detailed, cannot compete with the magnificence and beauty of Bauer's work. Drawings still tell deeper truths about botany than photography can, and in the twenty-first century Aljos Farjon's deceptively simple line drawings show the essence of pine tree species in variety, detail and elegance.

In contrast, Chinese culture has long regarded pines as important subjects. Here, their associations were quite different from those of Europe. In China, pines have long been admired for the resilient, twisted shapes they acquire with age and their beauty generally, as symbols of wisdom, longevity, hospitality and endurance, and as landscape features. An association of pine trees with human old age in Chinese culture is so deep that 'pine tree care' provides an Internet address for a large Chinese care-home group. As a symbol of hospitality, one of the best-known living Chinese trees is the Guest Welcoming Pine at Huangshan, an area famous for precipitous mountain scenery with pines growing from almost-vertical rock slopes. It is one of many named pine trees in the area. Korean and Japanese culture shared the tradition of venerating and naming individual pines.

Representations of pine trees are common in Chinese art. From the ninth century onwards, Chinese landscape painting developed the form most Westerners think of, with a wash evoking a misty landscape and sharper brushstrokes using ink to add trees, mountains and birds, buildings or other details. The principles of harmony, respect, purity and tranquillity that underlie this give an aesthetic in which the eye fills in the spaces. As common features of the Chinese landscape that also had deep spiritual significance, pine trees appear in a very high proportion of these images.

Combined with bamboo and plum blossoms, pine foliage is one of the 'three friends of winter', a trio used in compositions found as far back as the ninth century in both Chinese and Japanese art. Pine and bamboo are evergreen, and prunus blossom opens early in the year, so together they provide an auspicious gathering that symbolizes long life, strength, endurance and hope. Combinations in special arrangements with other plants, animals or rocks also have symbolic meanings, often relating to marital fidelity.[19]

Cakes of Chinese ink, moulded with patterns depicting pine trees and dragons and gilded, late 18th or early 19th century.

Ting Ying-Tsung, untitled woodcut of pine tree, plum and bamboo, 17th century.

Pines have a similar importance in Japan, both in life and in art.

> They are a symbol of longevity . . . evoking wisdom and knowl-
> edge. They are resistant to change, remaining evergreen
> through the turning seasons, and they are strong against
> the elements.[20]

The different growth habits of pine species – Japanese red pine, with
relatively soft foliage and smooth bark, and Japanese black pine, with
stiff needles and rough bark – are considered feminine and mascu-
line respectively. In Japanese culture, the needles of two-needled pines
can stand for marital fidelity, and the twin pines of Sumiyoshi and
Takasago, across from each other on Osaka Bay, are personified in
legend by an aged couple, the man from Sumiyoshi visiting the old
woman of Takasago daily. Pine has special associations with the New
Year, when bamboo and pine decorations, *kadomatsu*, are placed one on
either side of entrances, welcoming the gods into the houses.[21] The

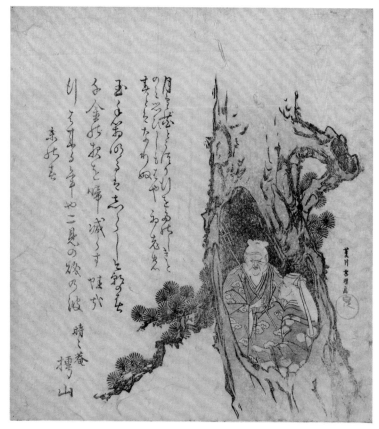

Hokusai Katsushika, *Tagasago Couple in the Hollow of a Pine Tree*, 1811, woodcut. In Japan, pines have been a symbol of marital fidelity since at least the 14th century, when a *Noh* play told of the two pines whose human personifications met each night.

link with the New Year is an old one that has carried into the twenty-first century, even though the date of the celebration has changed to 1 January from the Chinese lunar calendar, according to which the New Year fell between late January and mid-February.

The Japanese adhered to a similar zodiac system, applied to both years and individual days. At New Year, they observed a custom of collecting herbs for soup, and at the same time uprooting seedling pines. This gesture (dating back to at least the eighth century) was believed to encourage longevity. It took place on the year's first Day of the Rat, and was especially powerful if this coincided with the first day of the New Year. The custom is mentioned in the early eleventh-century Japanese *Tale of Genji*, in which the hero, the nobleman Genji, finds his daughter's page girls and maids 'playing about on the garden hill, uprooting seedling pines' on New Year's Day.[22] Pine branches were also attached to New Year's gifts; their overt meaning was good wishes for longevity, but also indicated children, seedling pines. In Japanese, *matsu*, the sound of the word used for pine tree, also sounds like the word used for the verb 'to wait', allowing much word play in poetry between lovers punning on the imagery of the trees and the notion of awaiting someone. Conveniently for English translators of Japanese poetry using pine-tree metaphors, the English verb 'to pine for' also carries a notion of waiting, allowing some of the sense in the original Japanese to be conveyed.

In Japan as in China, pine trees are a major feature of the landscape, carrying deeper meanings of longevity and endurance, and are frequent subjects in art. Pine-tree forms are often represented with foliage in cumulus-like shapes arranged in horizontal layers and slender vertical trunks. These are about the 'essence' of the trees

Hokusai Katsushika, *Komatsubiki* (Gathering Young Pine), 1804–07, woodcut. Picking young pine trees was considered an auspicious act in ancient Japanese belief.

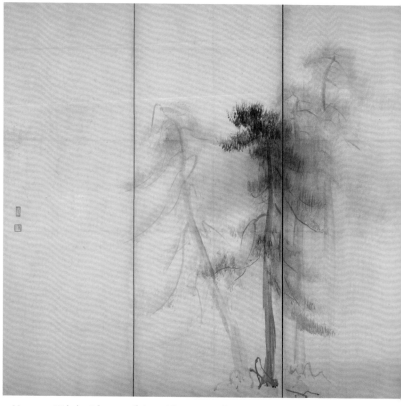

Hasegawa Tohaku, *The Forest of Pines*, 16th century, ink on paper. Artists in China and Japan were fascinated by the appearance of pine trees in mist long before Europeans began representing such scenes. This Japanese example is on a pair of folding screens.

rather than individual trees or places; their apparent effortlessness shows a reality quite unlike that seen in the works of European painters. Pine trees can be seen in scroll paintings and on lacquer and ceramics. *Hamamatsu*, representations of Japanese black pines by the shore, are especially striking. The theme is thought to have emerged over a thousand years ago in the Heian period (794–1185). A particularly beautiful example in the National Museum of Australia dates from about 1550. The trees spread from right to centre left, irregular but repeating forms floating across gold leaf. A band of blue across the lower centre represents the sea, with two small white boats balancing a group of horses depicted among the trees. The work is as sophisticated

— and considerably more peaceful than — Botticelli's *Decameron* scenes set amid the Ravenna pines, but both tell truths about the trees, their tranquillity, shapes and enduring indifference to the transient world of humans. Stylized representations of pine trees on folding screens in turn have influenced real trees that have been trained to represent the shapes portrayed by the screen artists.[23]

Gardeners in the Far East have made by far the most striking uses of pines in horticulture. Lacebark pines have long been a feature of Chinese temple courtyards. With age, their bark becomes a gleaming white, visible from a long way off, and individual trees are esteemed for their age, beauty and the shade they give. Zhang Zhu, a Yuan Dynasty poet, wrote about this tree:

Its pine needles as fine
As silver hairpins, . . .
By the temple, in misty rain,
It appears as a tall white dragon.[24]

The Chinese were also the originators of *penjing*, the art of grow-ing trees in restricted spaces so that although they are mature in shape they are dwarfed in stature. This is better known to Westerners under the Japanese name of bonsai, where the numerous pine tree forms show in miniatures, such as Japanese white pines with tiny needles upturned in bunches, the trunk carefully and gracefully trained in a zigzag series of 45-degree angles, or, in contrast, Japanese black pine, very squat with a trunk at once tiny and massive, the roots curv-ing out to grasp the soil and the upturned branches bearing tufts of (relatively) long needles.

Japanese gardens are inextricably linked to the country's landscapes, religious beliefs and aesthetics, and they are full of pines to the extent that these can be regarded as the tree type that defines them.[25] *Niwaki* pines (garden trees grown through a process of pruning and shaping, sometimes called 'cloud pruning' in English) are skillfully trained to produce a cultural artefact 'coaxing out those features believed to sig-nify "the essence of the tree": gnarled trunks, outstretched branches, rounded canopies'.[26]

Niwaki-trained pines are a feature of Ritsurin-koen, formerly a private garden but now a public park.

It is the pines . . . which that make this garden exceptional –
they are everywhere you look, clustered together on islands,
scrambling up slopes, forming long, caterpillar-like hedges,
framing views and leaning out over ponds.[27]

Skilled perspective tricks with rocks, gravel and mounds make 1.5-m-high pines appear like tall mountain trees when viewed from a distance. Curves or kinks are induced in the trunks, and lower

Hokusai Katsushika, *Man Sweeping Pine Needles that have Fallen from a Tree Near a Stone Shrine*, 1830–50, drawing. In Far Eastern art, the sprays of needles radiating from individual branches are commonly depicted in pictures of pine trees.

branches are removed and upper ones trained to be straight and horizontal, or into zigzags.

Patterns relating to pine trees are also frequent in Japanese textiles. Some are direct transfers of landscape painting techniques onto silk garments, while others show stylized pine patterns such as glittery winter scenes on black, or firework-like explosions of bunches of long needles leaving branches. Simple prints show *matsuba* — pine needles — in pairs just as they appear on the forest floor. A similar pattern is found in *sashiko* (a type of white-on-indigo stitching). A set of colours is used to represent pine trees on printed fabrics, principally deep greens, orange and rusty-red. Woven textiles display sophisticated patterns, including damask-type techniques; an example of a geisha's obi (wide kimono belt) displays the ends of branches showing buds against whorls of leaves, executed in pale gold damask weave on cream silk.[28] For those who had to suffer the mid-twentieth-century English use of 'pine' or 'forest' – dull, dark green – for school uniforms, they are a revelation.

In North America, much of the pre-Columbian symbolism relating to pine trees has either been lost or still lies buried in notes made by ethnographers. Colorado pinyon was an important part of the indigenous culture. In a gesture that recalls Japanese traditions of relating young children to sapling pines, Apache mothers would place the cradleboards of their children in the east sides of young pinyons, saying to a tree, 'Here is the baby carrier. I give this to you, still young and growing. I want my child to grow up as you do.' The Navajo followed a similar custom, although it was a dead child's cradleboard that was placed in the tree, with the cradle laces of a healthy child. Male initiation ceremonies involved placing ritual items in young pinyon pines. Their burning pitch provided incense, and ceremonial wands were made from branches selected from the cardinal points.[29]

Modern Western pine symbolism cannot match Far Eastern or ancient European myth for vivid imagery, and relates more to the economic importance of pines and their part in the natural world. A pine cone (from a Roman stone original) has long been a symbol for Augsburg (Bavaria), on seals for bolts of cloth, and as a silver mark, but the use of pine trees in colonial culture in North America is more clearly related to politics and trade. They appear on coins from New England in the seventeenth and eighteenth centuries and on state flags, and also as a pattern in quilting. The Vermont state seal bears the likeness of a pine tree with fourteen branches representing the original thirteen counties plus Vermont. Eastern white pine is the official tree of Maine, 'the pine-tree state', and appears on the state seal and the state flag, adopted because of an abundance of timber for shipbuilding in colonial times. The official state tree of Alabama is the longleaf pine, adopted in 1997.

In North America, an alternative method of exploring the forms and landscapes of pine trees produced some of the most beautiful and

Colour lithograph after a painting by Andrew Melrose, *c.* 1887, *Yosemite Valley from Mariposa Trail.* Exploration of the granite scenery and conifer forests of Yosemite Valley in California by people of European origin began in the 1850s. Artists, poets, photographers and early environmentalists were all fascinated by the area.

enduring images. Photography brought to the public consciousness both the scale of industrial logging, in hundreds of newspaper and publicity photographs, and the sublime landscape of the American southwest. The Yosemite Valley was especially important, a subject for photography as early as 1861, when Carleton Watkins carried his heavy plate camera into the mountains and began photographing scenery and treescapes. The images he made were exhibited in New York in 1862 and were a major factor in legislation signed by Abraham Lincoln in 1863, which effectively made the valley a national park, securing it as a public amenity, unavailable to mining and logging companies.[30]

These photographs were precursors of the work of Ansel Adams (1902–1984), who was famous for his photographs of the area. His black-and-white images of sky, water and spectacular mountains, and his detailed studies, including many of pines, helped to shape a view of Yosemite. Close-ups show subjects such as the ends of pine-tree boughs, their needles as slender black fans emerging from a mass of snow, pine cones, and the grain of worn and twisted dead trees that have lost their bark. More distant views place the trees in their forest environment, as tangled, snow-laden boughs against other trees, open tree crowns in massive mountain landscapes, weather-worn trunks whose tough verticality contrasts with the apparent softness of white water spilling over a massive fall, or spires spilling down glaciated valleys. Adams plays with perspective, making pines of the typical conifer shape seem taller than the conical mountain that appears behind them, or picturing a tree in the foreground melting into a row of other pines high on a distant ledge. At times they are small, dark isosceles triangles, whose curving distribution across a sweep of dipping mountainside emphasizes the spectacular geology of Yosemite.[31]

The bristlecone pines seem to be the ones that have most fascinated the Western world recently. Michael Cohen considers their aesthetics in *A Garden of Bristlecones*; he discusses how age and weather, especially winds laden with snow and particles of sand, have shaped the wood of these ancient trees.

> Aesthetic qualities of groves and individuals are created by the prevailing wind, which is also the direction from which the light flows. On a bright morning when they seem created by light, this is not an illusion. . . . Wind, cold and light seem to conspire at timberline, creating a certain order among trees.[32]

Cohen comments how the individual trees seem alike but different at the same time, how light on the dead wood attracts photographers, so that they miss the fact that the lee sides of the trees are often a mass of foliage, whose surface presents an evenness that is problematic for the artist, as is tension between 'complexity and abstraction' when the trees are viewed from a distance. In a meditation on the forms of the trees in their differing environments (there are several groves, on differing rock formations), his wife considers their forms, their horizontals, verticals and curves as seen from a distance and close to, and their overall conical form together with differences in light values between lit wood, shadows and dark foliage.

Contemporary attitudes to bristlecone pines seem to reflect something of the Far Eastern respect for the longevity of pines. Cohen remarks how a sense that cutting down a bristlecone is a sin became common in the 1990s, the debate seeming to relate to the significance of the wood that has 'acquired importance beyond curiosity'.[33] A combination of their intriguing visual appearance combined with awe for their great age (perhaps particularly important in a country whose colonial history is short and which has cut down vast numbers of ancient trees) seems to be at work here.

seven

The Sound of the Wind
in the Branches

J ohn Evelyn lived in a world untroubled by Romantic sensibilities. 'The next morning', he wrote in his diary on a northwards journey over the Alps to Briga,

> we mounted again through strange, horrid and fearful crags and tracts, abounding in pine-trees, and inhabited only by bears, wolves and wild goats; nor could we see anywhere above a pistol-shot before us, the horizon being terminated with rocks and mountains, whose tops, covered with snow, appeared to touch the skies and in many places pierced the clouds.[1]

Mountains made life difficult, wild animals were dangerous and pine trees, in Evelyn's book *Sylva, or a Discourse of Forest-Trees*, were the subject of cultivation with an eye to their utility.

In *The Mysteries of Udolpho* (1794), Ann Radcliffe sent Emily travelling through a mountainous landscape, 'the Appenines in their darkest horrors . . . the long perspective of retiring summits rising over each other, their ridges clothed with pines', as she is borne towards the Castle of Udolpho, 'silent, lonely and sublime'.[2] The notion of the sublime and the sensibilities of the Romantic Movement ultimately led to the non-utilitarian view of nature, which found its apotheosis in the scenery of western North America. One of the most influential writers on this was the Scottish-born naturalist John Muir. A prolific writer of prose and journalism, he was captivated by the dramatic

Engraving by A. H. Payne after a picture by W. Rahl, 1845, *Schloss Krempenstein.*
The influence of the Romantic movement changed opinions on mountain scenery
and conifer forests from an uncomfortable obstacle to travel destinations admired
for their atmosphere.

landscapes of the west-coast mountains and the Yosemite Valley,
about which he wrote extensively. 'God's big show' provided him
with ample material:

> I wish you could see our pines in full bloom of soft snow
> or waving in a storm. They know little of the character of a
> pine tree who see it only when swaying drowsily in a sum-
> mer breeze or when balanced motionless and fast asleep in
> hushed sunshine.[3]

He recorded his experiences, which would touch any romantic:

> In the evening Black and I rode together up into the sugar pine
> forests and onto his old ranch in the moonlight. The grand
> priest-like pines held their arms above those in blessing. The
> wind sang songs of welcome. The cruel glaciers and the run-
> ning crystal fountains were in it. . . . pine tasselled overarching
> and brushing both cheeks at once . . . About eight o'clock a

Tom Thomson, *The Jack Pine*, 1916–17, oil on canvas. Paintings by the Canadian Group of Seven artists were influenced by Japanese prints and helped to shape Canadian sensibilities about pine trees and their place in the landscape.

strange mass of tones came surging and waving through the pines. 'That's the death song,' said Black, as he reigned up his horse to listen. 'Some Indian is dead.'[4]

Muir's admiration for the pines was unbounded. 'Lambertiana [sugar pine] is easily King of all the world-wide realm of pines, while Ponderosa is the noble, unconquerable mailed knight, without fear and without reproach.'[5] Entranced by the environment and the trees of the Sierra Nevada, he became what would now be called an environmental activist. He helped establish the Yosemite and Sequoia National Parks in the early 1890s, as well as the National Forest land classification, which stipulates the management regimes of specified areas, and co-founded the Sierra Club, still an influential campaigning organization for the natural environment in the USA.

Many echoed Muir's love of pine trees. One was Robert Service (1874–1958), also of Scottish extraction, who spent his early career in western Canada, publishing many poems relating to the people and environment he found there. In 'Dark Pine' the poet wishes for his soul to inhabit a pine tree after death:

Aye, when my soul shall sally forth
Let it be to the naked North,
And in a lone pine desolate
Achieve its fit and final fate;
A pine by arctic tempest torn,
Snow-scourged, wind-savaged and forlorn;
A Viking trunk, a warrior tree,
A hostage to dark destiny
Of iron earth and icy sky,
That valiantly disdains to die.

There is the home where I would bide,
If trees like men had souls inside,–
Which is, of course, a fantasy
None could conceive but dolts like me. . .

Let others vision Heaven's Gate,
Dark Pine, I dream for me you wait.[6]

Service expresses the nature of pine trees in full Romantic flow, celebrating their tenacity, their ability to grow in unpromising places, soils and climates, their longevity and the manner in which individual trees can stand as landmarks in the wilderness.

Poets are the only observers who mention a minor but important aspect of pines: the sound the wind makes when it blows through their boughs. Perhaps this sighing was behind the myth of Pitys and Boreas. Virgil mentioned that

The hill of Menelaus has whispering pines,
And all its pine trees sing.
It hears the loves
Of shepherds and the ancient pipes of Pan.[7]

Although Whispering Pines later became a clichéd name for houses and other property, especially in North America, the notion of the pines singing or talking recurs in poetry. 'Shaking their Choral locks', said Leigh Hunt, referring to the noise made by the pines of Ravenna.[8]

The sounds made by pine trees also intrigued the Chinese, who made numerous references to them in their poetry. 'The Song of the Wind Through the Pines' is the name of a melody for the qin (a Chinese stringed instrument of ancient origin), often connected with a famous musician Xi Kang (233–262). A lyric for the music mentions:

1,000 branches and 10,000 leaves in the wind sough,
A wonderful person takes his qin and his playing forms
    a song,
Creating amongst the pines sounds both brief and long,[9]

carrying the notion of harmony between the music and the trees. There are numerous other examples, including 'Climbing up the Cold Mountain', which describes a rough mountain path with a sense of mystery: of moss that is slippery without rain, and of pine trees that sing without wind.[10]

The poetic notion of sound from pine trees was mentioned by Longfellow more than once, for instance in 'Evangeline' (1847), the story of an Acadian girl searching for her lost love across the landscapes of America:

This is the forest primeval. The murmuring pines and the
    hemlocks,
bearded with moss, and in garments green, indistinct in
    the twilight . . .[11]

Ma Lin, *Listening to the Wind in Pines*, 13th century, ink and colours on silk. The characteristic sounds made by the wind blowing through pine boughs have mostly been the subject of myth and poetry. They are especially important in Chinese poems.

although his use of strong metre somewhat subdued the notion in
The Song of Hiawatha (1855):

Round about the Indian village
spread the meadows and the cornfields
and beyond them stood the forest,

東海道
五拾三次
之内

吉原
左冨士

Hiroshige Ando, *Yoshiwara*, 1833–6, woodcut. Pine trees line a narrow road between two stretches of water in a scene from Japan.

Hanging scroll, by an unknown Chinese artist, showing a pine tree, bamboo, rock and fungus, late 16th or early 17th century, ink and colours on paper.

stood the groves of singing pine trees,
Green in summer, white in winter,
ever sighing, ever singing . . .[12]

His English contemporary Barry Cornwall (pseudonym for Bryon Waller Procter, 1787–1874) was also taken by the noise of the pines:

With such a noise
As the rough winds of all to make when they
Pass o'er a forest, and bend down the Pines . . .[13]

and talks of 'Funereal Cypress, Yew, and shadowy Pine, dark trees', that

At night
Shook from their melancholy branches sounds
And sighs like death.[14]

Different species apparently make different noises as the breeze blows through them, Michael Cohen commenting that among bristlecone pines 'Moving air brings out low notes, and none of the whistling heard in forests of long-leaved pines.'[15] The sound has enchanted musicians as well, most notably the composer Ottorino Respighi (1879–1936), whose work *Pines of Rome* is one of three orchestral tone poems reflecting the soundscape of the city.[16]

Ralph Waldo Emerson's poem 'Woodnotes II', exploring his ideas about Transcendentalism, placed the pine tree centrally as subject and narrator, telling of its ability to resist adversity and making a plea for humanity to listen:

Heed the old oracles,
Ponder my spells;
Song wakes in my pinnacles
When the wind swells.
Soundeth the prophetic wind,

The shadows shake on the rock behind,
And the countless leaves of the pine are strings
Tuned to the lay the wood-god sings.
Hearken! Hearken![17]

This ancient, tenacious and adaptable genus of trees has withstood
eons of time, of tectonic and climatic change. It has successfully
adapted to numerous different environments, enduring in places
where many other trees give up, and at the same time developing species
of great individuality. The symbolism of pine trees runs deep in many
cultures. Their wood supplied humans with warmth and light, and
together with resin helped shape life in many parts of the northern
hemisphere before the advent of hydrocarbon fuels; perhaps it will
be useful once again in the future. We should treasure, respect and
listen to the pine trees.

Timeline

c. 130 million years ago	Cretaceous: *Pinus belgica*, earliest known pine fossil
c. 75 million : years ago	pines differentiated into hard and soft types
c. 15,000 BC	charcoal from *P. pinaster* in Lascaux cave
c. 8000 BC	evidence for pinewood posts at site later occupied by Stonehenge
c. 7500 BC	early inhabitants of USA use seeds from pinyons and other pines as food
c. 4000 BC	eradication of Scots pine in most of Britain through demand for timber and charcoal especially for smelting
c. 2700 BC	Germination of 'Methuselah', the oldest known living single organism, in the Great Basin of Colorado
c. 300 BC	Theophrastus describes pine trees and their uses
900–1200 AD	Anasazi settlements in North America make extensive use of *P. ponderosa* for building
960–1127	Northern Song Dynasty landscape painting includes many representations of pines
1643	Wood Tar Company of Stockholm founded

1704	An Act for Encouraging the Importation of Naval Stores from America passed by the English government, leading to the 'Broad Arrow' policy in New England
1713	*P. pinaster* used to stabilize dunes in southwest France
1753	Linnaeus names ten species in genus *Pinus*
1775–83	American War of Independence affects British supplies of tar and naval stores
1802	Aylmer Bourke Lambert publishes *A Description of the Genus Pinus*, the first monograph on pines
1830s	The rubber industry starts using turpentine as a solvent
1845	Rapid expansion in coal-tar distilling, replacing many pine products
1870s	Development of Kraft paper process (alkaline)
1893	Koehne proposes division of genus *Pinus* into *haploxylon* and *diploxylon*, based on presence of one or two vascular bundles
Early 1900s	Development of Masonite hardboard from wood pulp and bark chips
1905	Courtaulds begin producing viscose rayon commercially
1937	Laurel and Hardy include 'The Trail of the Lonesome Pine' in their film *Way Out West*.
Late 1940s	Arizona Chemical Co. develops fractional distillation process for separating tall oil
1990s	Clade analysis becomes a dominant method for evolutionary classification, leading to revisions in thought about relationships between pine species
2001	The television series *The Sopranos* uses the Pine Barrens as a setting

References

Introduction

1 Aljos Farjon, *Pines: Drawings and Descriptions of the Genus Pinus* (Leiden, 2005); James E. Eckenwalder, *Conifers of the World: The Complete Reference* (Portland, OR, 2009).
2 Eckenwalder, *Conifers of the World*, p. 480.
3 David M. Richardson, ed., *Ecology and Biogeography of Pinus* (Cambridge, 1998), p. 38.

1 The Natural History of Pine Trees

1 Pierre Pomet, *A Compleat History of Druggs*, 3rd edn (London, 1737), p. 146.
2 Aljos Farjon, *Pines: Drawings and Descriptions of the Genus Pinus*, 2nd edn (Leiden, 2005), p. 220.
3 William Frederic Badè, ed., *Life and Letters of John Muir* (Boston, MA, 1924), vol. II, p. 116.
4 Pomet, *History of Druggs*, p. 146.
5 Ibid., p. 146.
6 Stephen Elliott, *A Sketch of the Botany of South Carolina and Georgia* (Charleston, SC, 1824), vol. II, p. 636.
7 Farjon, *Pines*, p. 15.
8 John Claudius Loudon, *An Encylopaedia of Trees and Shrubs, Being the Arboretum et Fructicetum Britannicum Abridged* (London, 1842), p. 970.
9 Ronald M. Lanner, *The Bristlecone Book: A Natural History of the World's Oldest Trees* (Missoula, MT, 2007), p. 29.
10 Farjon, *Pines*, p. 35.
11 Ronald M. Lanner, *The Piñon Pine: A Natural and Cultural History* (Reno, NV, 1981), p. 53.
12 Farjon, *Pines*, p. 21.
13 Nicholas T. Mirov and Jean Hasbrouck, *The Story of Pines* (Bloomington, IN, and London, 1976), pp. 34–5.
14 Lanner, *The Bristlecone Book*, p. 33.

15 Mirov and Hasbrouck, *The Story of Pines*, p. 36.
16 Ibid., p. 10.
17 Mary Curry Tressider, *Trees of Yosemite: A Popular Account* (Stanford, CA, 1932), p. 43.
18 John Davies, *Douglas of the Forests: The North American Journals of David Douglas* (Edinburgh, 1979), p. 103.
19 P. G. Walsh, ed., *Pliny the Younger: Complete Letters* (Oxford, 2006), p. 143.
20 James E. Cole, 'The Cone-Bearing Trees of Yosemite National Park', *Yosemite Nature Notes*, XVIII/5 (Yosemite, CA, 1939), p. 13.
21 Ibid., p. 19.
22 Robert Seymour and Malcolm L. Hunter, 'Principles of Ecological Forestry', in *Maintaining Biodiversity in Forest Ecosystems*, ed. Malcolm L. Hunter (Cambridge, 1999), p. 33.
23 John McPhee, *The Pine Barrens* (New York, 1968), p. 111.
24 Chris Czajkowski, personal communication, 30 July 2004.
25 Robert B. Outland III, *Tapping the Pines: The Naval Stores Industry in the American South* (Baton Rouge, LA, 2004), pp. 16–18.
26 John Evelyn, *Sylva, or a Discourse of Forest Trees and the Propogation of Timber: A Reprint of the 4th edn of 1716* (London, 1908), vol. I, p. 229.
27 Loudon, *An Encylopaedia of Trees and Shrubs*, p. 948.
28 Lanner, *The Bristlecone Book*, p. 86.
29 Peter B. Lavery and Donald J. Mead, '*Pinus radiata*: A Narrow Endemic from North America Takes On the World', in *Ecology and Biogeography of Pinus*, ed. David M. Richardson (Cambridge, 1998), p. 447.
30 Marcel Barbero, Roger Loisel, Pierre Quézel, David M. Richardson and François Romane, 'Pines of the Mediterranean Basin', in *Ecology and Biogeography of Pinus*, ed. Richardson, pp. 153–70.
31 D. C. Le Maitre, 'Pines in Cultivation', in *Ecology and Biogeography of Pinus*, ed. Richardson, p. 412–13.
32 Aljos Farjon, *A Natural History of Conifers* (Portland, OR, 2008), p. 68.
33 Constance I. Millar, 'Early Evolution of Pines', in *Ecology and Biogeography of Pinus*, ed. Richardson, pp. 69–95.
34 Farjon, *Pines*, p. 181.
35 Katherine J. Willis, Keith D. Bennett and H. John Birks, 'The Late Quaternary Dynamics of Pines in Europe', in *Ecology and Biogeography of Pinus*, ed. Richardson, pp. 107–21.
36 John Ingram Lockhart, trans., *The Memoirs of the Conquistador Bernal Díaz del Castillio* (London, 1844), vol. I, p. 139.
37 Jesse P. Perry, *The Pines of Mexico and Central America* (Portland, OR, 1991), p. 217.
38 George Russell Shaw, *The Pines of Mexico* (Boston, MA, 1909), p. 3.
39 Farjon, *Pines*, p. 117.
40 Nicholas T. Mirov, *The Genus Pinus* (New York, 1967), pp. 11–12.
41 Shaw, *The Pines of Mexico*, p. 1.
42 Perry, *The Pines of Mexico and Central America*, p. 22.
43 Ibid., p. 217.

2 Pine Trees in Myth and Reality

1 A. S. Kline, trans., *Ovid: The Metamorphoses*, www.ovid.lib.virginia.edu, Book VI: 675–721.

2 Aaron J. Atsma, 'Flora 2: Plants of Greek Myth: Pine, Corsican and Pine, Stone' (2000–2001), www.theoi.com.

3 Nicholas T. Mirov, *The Genus Pinus* (New York, 1967), p. 4.

4 Nicholas T. Mirov and Jean Hasbrouck, *The Story of Pines* (Bloomington, IN, and London, 1976), p. 137.

5 Alan Davidson, *Oxford Companion to Food*, 2nd edn (Oxford, 2006), p. 608.

6 Mirov, *The Genus Pinus*, p. 19.

7 Sir Arthur Hort, trans., *Theophrastus: Enquiry into Plants and Minor Works on Odours and Weather Signs* (London, 1916), vol. I, p. xiii.

8 Ibid., p. 211.

9 Ibid., p. 217.

10 Ibid., p. 213.

11 Russell Meiggs, *Trees and Timber in the Ancient Mediterranean World* (Oxford, 1982), pp. 43–4.

12 Christian A. Daniels and Nicholas K. Menzies, *Agroindustries and Forestry* (Cambridge, 1996), *Science and Civilisation in China*, vol. VI, pt 3, p. 600.

13 Ibid., pp. 568–70.

14 Mirov, *The Genus Pinus*, pp. 7–8.

15 Pierre Pomet, *A Compleat History of Druggs*, 3rd edn (London, 1737), p. 146.

16 Mirov, *The Genus Pinus*, p. 9.

17 Ibid., p. 10.

18 Aljos Farjon, *Pines: Drawings and Descriptions of the Genus Pinus*, 2nd edn (Leiden, 2005), p. 218.

19 James Robertson, *A Naturalist in the Highlands*, ed. D. M. Henderson and J. H. Dickinson (Edinburgh, 1994), p. 159.

20 Aylmer B. Lambert, *A Description of the Genus Pinus* (London, 1803), preface.

21 William T. Stearn, 'Lambert, Aylmer Bourke (1761–1842)', *Oxford Dictionary of National Biography* (Oxford, 2004), www.oxforddnb.com.

22 John Davies, *Douglas of the Forests: The North American Journals of David Douglas* (Edinburgh, 1980), p. 103.

23 John Hillier and Allen Coombes, eds, *The Hillier Manual of Trees and Shrubs* (Newton Abbott, 2007), p. 462.

24 Anon., *Pinus strobus*, USDA Forest Service Technology Transfer Factsheet (Madison, WI, n.d.), p. 1.

25 Robert A. Price, Aaron Liston and Steven H. Strauss, 'Phylogeny and Systematics of *Pinus*', in *Ecology and Biogeography of Pinus*, ed. David M. Richardson (Cambridge, 1998).

26 Ibid., p. 51.

27 Quoted in Mirov, *The Genus Pinus*, p. 12.

28 Farjon, *Pines*, p. 11.

29 Ibid., pp. 11–12.

30 Ibid., p. 220.

3 Pitch, Turpentine and Rosin

1 Joseph Needham with Ho Ping-Yu and Lu Gwei-Djen, *Spagyrical Discovery and Invention: Historical Survey from Cinnabar Elixirs to Synthetic Insulin* (Cambridge, 1976), in series *Science and Civilisation in China*, vol. V, pt 3, sect. 33, pp. 33, 235.
2 Russell Meiggs, *Trees and Timber in the Ancient Mediterranean World* (Oxford, 1982), p. 467.
3 Robert B. Outland III, *Tapping the Pines: The Naval Stores Industry in the American South* (Baton Rouge, LA, 2004), pp. 5–6.
4 Nicholas T. Mirov, *Composition of Gum Turpentines of Pines* (Washington, DC, 1961), p. 157.
5 Outland III, *Tapping the Pines*, p. 175.
6 Sir Arthur Hort, trans., *Theophrastus: Enquiry into Plants and Minor Works on Odours and Weather Signs* (London, 1916), vol. II, p. 225.
7 Ibid., pp. 229–33.
8 Pierre Pomet, *A Compleat History of Druggs*, 3rd edn (London, 1737), p. 212.
9 John Evelyn, *Sylva, or a Discourse of Forest Trees and the Propagation of Timber: A Reprint of the 4th edn. of 1716* (London, 1908), vol. I, pp. 246–7.
10 Thomas Gamble, 'How the Famous Stockholm Tar of Centuries Renown is Made', in *Naval Stores: History, Production, Distribution and Consumption*, ed. Thomas Gamble (Savannah, GA, 1921), pp. 57–9.
11 John William Humphrey, John Peter Olson and Andrew N. Sherwood, *Greek and Roman Technology: A Sourcebook* (London, 1998), pp. 345–6.
12 E. S. Forster and Edward H. Heffner, trans., *Lucius Junius Moderatus Columella on Agriculture and Trees* (Cambridge, MA, 1955), vol. III, pp. 227–45.
13 Humphrey, *Greek and Roman Technology*, p. 345.
14 Forster, *Columella on Agriculture and Trees*, p. 227.
15 Ibid., p. 243.
16 Ibid., p. 237.
17 Andrew Dalby, trans., *Geoponika: Farm Work* (Totnes, 2011), pp. 150–05.
18 Ibid., p. 313.
19 Lu Gwei-Djen and Huang Hsing-Tsung, *Botany* (Cambridge, 1986), in series *Science and Civilisation in China*, vol. VI, pt 1, pp. 482.
20 Ho Ping-Yu, Lu Gwei-Djen and Wang Ling, *Military Technology: The Gunpowder Epic* (Cambridge, 1987), in series *Science and Civilisation in China*, vol. V, pt 7, pp. 260–01.
21 Evelyn, *Sylva, or a Discourse of Forest Trees*, p. 249.
22 Pomet, *History of Druggs*, p. 212.
23 Ann Lindsay Mitchell and Syd House, *David Douglas: Explorer and Botanist* (London, 1999), p.124.
24 Humphrey, *Greek and Roman Technology*, p. 346.
25 Pomet, *History of Druggs*, p. 212.
26 Theodore P. Kaye, 'Pine Tar, History and Uses' (San Francisco, CA, 1997), available at www.maritime.org.
27 Outland III, *Tapping the Pines*, p. 9.

28 Ibid., p. 13.
29 Pomet, *History of Druggs*, p. 209.
30 Ibid., p. 210.
31 John Davies, *A Manual of Materia Medica and Pharmacy* (London, 1831),
    p. 191.
32 Pomet, *History of Druggs*, p. 211.
33 C. Anne Wilson, *Water of Life: A History of Wine, Distilling and Spirits 300
    BC–2000 AD* (Totnes, 2006), pp. 35–9.
34 Outland III, *Tapping the Pines*, p. 76.
35 See ibid., pp. 68–9, for a detailed description of this and the following
    process.
36 Quoted in Dana F. White and Victor A. Kramer, *Olmstead South: Old South
    Critic, New South Planner* (Westport, CT, 1979), p. 55.
37 James E. Eckenwalder, *Conifers of the World: The Complete Reference* (Portland,
    OR, 2009), p. 459.
38 J. J. W. Coppen and G. A. Hone, *Gum Naval Stores: Turpentine and Rosin from
    Pine Resin* (Rome, 1995), ch. 1, www.fao.org.
39 Pomet, *History of Druggs*, p. 213.
40 Robert Latham and William Matthews, eds, *The Diary of Samuel Pepys*
    (Berkeley and Los Angeles, CA, 2000), vol. V, p. 1.
41 Davies, *A Manual of Materia Medica*, p. 192.
42 Pomet, *History of Druggs*, p. 211.
43 Outland III, *Tapping the Pines* pp. 159–60.
44 Nicholas T. Mirov and Jean Hasbrouck, *The Story of Pines* (Bloomington,
    IN, and London, 1976), pp. 37–8.
45 William Bray, ed., *The Diary of John Evelyn* (New York and London, 1901),
    vol. II, p. 22.
46 Mirov, *The Genus Pinus*, p. 482.
47 Forestry Commission, 'Non-Timber Markets for Trees', n.d., at
    secure.fera.defra.gov.uk.
48 Coppen, *Gum Naval Stores*, ch. 1, available at www.fao.org.

4 Pine for Timber and Torches

 1 John Lindley and Thomas Moore, *The Treasury of Botany* (London, 1866),
    vol. II, p. 891.
 2 David Soulman, personal communication, 23 January 2011.
 3 Albert Brown Lyons, *Plant Names Scientific and Popular* (Detroit, MI, 1900),
    p. 291.
 4 Anon., 'Western Pine Versus Western White Pine', in *American
    Lumberman and Building Products Merchandiser*, 1775 (1909), p. 1180.
 5 John Claudius Loudon, *An Encyclopaedia of Trees and Shrubs, Being the Arboretum
    et Fructicetum Britannicum Abridged* (London, 1842), p. 952.
 6 Ibid., p. 1017.
 7 John Evelyn, *Sylva, or a Discourse of Forest Trees and the Propagation of Timber:
    A Reprint of the 4th edn. of 1716* (London, 1908), vol. I, pp. 240–41.

8 D. M. Henderson and J. H. Dickinson, eds, James Robertson, *A Naturalist in the Highlands* (Edinburgh, 1994), p. 166.
9 Quoted by Christian A. Daniels and Nicholas K. Menzies, *Agroindustries and Forestry* (Cambridge, 1996), *Science and Civilisation in China*, vol. VI, pt 3, p. 571.
10 George Russell Shaw, *The Genus Pinus* (Cambridge, MA, 1914), p. 48.
11 Francis Pryor, *The Making of the British Landscape* (London, 2010), p. 36.
12 Russell Meiggs, *Trees and Timber in the Ancient Mediterranean World* (Oxford, 1982), p. 37.
13 Ibid., p. 202.
14 Ibid., p. 241.
15 Evelyn, *Sylva, or a Discourse of Forest Trees,* , vol. I, p. 232.
16 Andrew Jackson Downing, *A Treatise on the Theory and Practice of Landscape Gardening Adapted to North America* (New York, 1856), p. 289.
17 James E. Cole, 'The Cone-Bearing Trees of Yosemite', *Yosemite Nature Notes*, XVIII/5 (1939), p. 22.
18 S. A. Barrett and E. W. Gifford, *Miwok Material Culture: Indian Life of the Yosemite Region: Dwellings* (Milwaukee, WI, 1933), available at www.yosemite.ca.us
19 S. A. Barrett and E. W. Gifford, *Miwok Material Culture: Indian Life of the Yosemite Region: Coiled Baskets* (Milwaukee, WI, 1933), available at www.yosemite.ca.us.
20 Evelyn, *Sylva, or a Discourse of Forest Trees*, vol. I, pp. 239–40.
21 Ibid., p. 241.
22 Loudon, *An Encylopaedia of Trees and Shrubs*, pp. 1018–19.
23 Ibid., p. 958.
24 Graeme Wynn, 'Timber Trade History', in *The Canadian Encyclopedia Online*, www.thecanadianencyclopedia.com, 2011.
25 Lady Strachey, ed., *Memoirs of a Highland Lady: The Autobiography of Elizabeth Grant of Rothiemurchus* (London, 1911), p. 219.
26 Ibid., pp. 221–2.
27 Wynn, 'Timber Trade History'.
28 Edward A. Goldman, 'Edward William Nelson, Naturalist 1855–1934', in *The Auk*, LII/2 (1935), pp. 137–8.
29 Stephen Elliott, *A Sketch of the Botany of South Carolina and Georgia* (Charleston, SC, 1824), vol. II, p. 638.
30 Ibid., p. 637.
31 Shaw, *The Genus Pinus*, p. 72.
32 Ibid., p. 74.
33 Ronald M. Lanner, *The Piñon Pine: A Natural and Cultural History* (Reno, NV, 1981), pp. 125–8.
34 Bohun B. Kinloch, *Sugar Pine: An American Wood,* USDA FS-257 (Washington, DC, 1984), pp. 5–6.
35 Rachel Feild, *Collector's Guide to Buying Antique Furniture* (London, 1988), pp. 38–9.
36 David Soulman, personal communication, 23 January 2011.
37 Elliott, *A Sketch of the Botany of South Carolina and Georgia*, p. 632.

38 David C. Le Maitre, 'Pines in Cultivation: A Global View', in *Ecology and Biogeography of Pinus*, ed. David M. Richardson (Cambridge, 1998), p. 415.
39 Herbet L. Edlin, *Know Your Conifers* (London, 1970), p. 10.
40 Le Maitre, 'Pines in Cultivation', in *Ecology and Biogeography of Pinus*, p. 416.
41 James E. Eckenwalder, *Conifers of the World: The Complete Reference* (Portland, OR, 2009), p. 470.
42 Ibid., p. 458.
43 Outland III, *Tapping the Pines: The Naval Stores Industry in the American South* (Baton Rouge, LA, 2004), pp. 102–05.
44 Constance Millar, 'Genetic Diversity', in *Maintaining Biodiversity in Forest Ecosystems*, ed. Malcolm L. Hunter (Cambridge, 1999), p. 482.
45 David Soulman, personal communication, 23 January 2011.
46 Forestry Commission, *Non-Timber Markets for Trees*, n.d., available at secure.fera.defra.gov.uk.
47 Ronald Lanner, *The Bristlecone Book: A Natural History of the World's Oldest Trees* (Missoula, MT, 2007), p. 18.
48 Shirley A. Graham, 'Anatomy of the Lindbergh Kidnapping', *Journal of Forensic Sciences*, XLII/3 (1997), pp. 368–77.
49 Evelyn, *Sylva, or a Discourse of Forest*, vol. I, p. 247.
50 Tsien Tsuen-Hsuin, *Paper and Printing* (Cambridge, 1985), *Science and Civilisation in China*, series vol. V, pt I, pp. 240–51.
51 Bettany Hughes, *The Hemlock Cup: Socrates, Athens and the Search for the Good Life* (London, 2011), pp. 368–71.
52 Phillip Vellacott, trans., *Euripides, Trojan Women*, 310ff., at www.theoi.com
53 Andrew Dalby, trans., *Geoponika: Farm Work* (Totnes, 2011), p. 306.
54 Strachey, *Memoirs of a Highland Lady*, p. 227.
55 George Russell Shaw, *The Pines of Mexico* (Boston, MA, 1909), p. 51.

5 Pine for Food

1 James E. Eckenwalder, *Conifers of the World: The Complete Reference* (Portland, OR, 2009), p. 447.
2 Gillian Riley, *The Oxford Companion to Italian Food* (London, 2007), pp. 404–05.
3 Ronald Lanner, *The Piñon Pine: A Natural and Cultural History* (Reno, NV, 1981), pp. 100–01.
4 US Food and Drug Administration, '"Pine Mouth" and Consumption of Pine Nuts', 14 March 2011, at www.fda.gov.
5 Frédéric Destaillats et al., 'Identification of the Botanical Origin of Commercial Pine Nuts Responsible for Dysgeusia by Gas-liquid Chromatography Analysis of Fatty Acid Profile', *Journal of Toxicology*, 2011 (2011), Article ID 316789, available at www.hindawi.com.
6 Pierre Pomet, *A Compleat History of Druggs*, 3rd edn (London, 1737), p. 146.
7 Yorgos Moussouris and Pedro Regato, 'Forest Harvest: An Overview of Non Timber Forest Products in the Mediterranean Region' (1999), at www.fao.org.

8 Chris Grocock and Sally Grainger, *Apicius: A Critical Edition with an Introduction and an English Translation of the Latin Recipe Text of Apicius* (Totnes, 2006), p. 149.
9 Claudia Roden, *A Book of Middle Eastern Food* (London, 1970), p. 235.
10 Claudia Roden, *The Food of Italy* (London, 1999), p. 54.
11 Riley, *Oxford Companion to Italian Food*, p. 388.
12 Peter Davidson and Jane Stevenson, eds, *The Closet of the Eminently Learned Sir Kenelm Digby Kt. Opened* (Totnes, 1997), p. 200.
13 Laura Mason, *Sugar Plums and Sherbet: The Prehistory of Sweets* (Totnes, 1998), p. 78.
14 Anon., *Brieve e nuovo modo da farsi ogni sorte di Sorbette con facilita* (Naples, n.d., *c.* 1690s); my thanks to Gillian Riley, Robin Weir and Ivan Day for this translation.
15 Anissa Helou, *Lebanese Cuisine* (London, 1994), pp. 248–9.
16 Ibid., pp. 27–8.
17 Quoted by D.C. Le Maitre, 'Pines in Cultivation', in *Ecology and Biogeography of Pinus*, ed. David M. Richardson (Cambridge, 1998), p. 409.
18 Alexander Gerard, *Account of Koonawur in the Himalaya* (London, 1841), pp. 226–7.
19 Nicholas T. Mirov and Jean Hasbrouck, *The Story of Pines* (Bloomington, IN, and London, 1976), p. 60.
20 Lanner, *The Piñon Pine*, p. 56.
21 Ibid., p 89.
22 Willis Linn Jepson, *The Trees of California* (San Francisco, CA, 1909), p. 36.
23 Lanner, *The Piñon Pine*, p. 58.
24 Ibid., p. 67
25 John Muir, *The Mountains of California* (New York, 1907), pp. 221–2.
26 Ibid., p. 219.
27 Ibid., p. 222.
28 Lanner, *The Piñon Pine*, p. 70.
29 S. A. Barrett and E. W. Gifford, *Miwok Material Culture: Indian Life of the Yosemite Region: Conifers* (Milwaukee, WI, 1933), available at www.yosemite.ca.us
30 Willis Linn Jepson, *The Trees of California*, pp. 37–8.
31 Barret, *Miwok Material Culture, Conifers*, available at www.yosemite.ca.us.
32 Le Maitre, 'Pines in Cultivation', p. 418.
33 Mary Isin, *Sherbet and Spice: The Complete Story of Turkish Sweets and Desserts* (London, 2012), p. 38.
34 Ibid., p. 39.
35 Quoted by Bohun B. Kinloch, *Sugar Pine: An American Wood*, USDA FS-257 (Washington, DC, 1984), p. 5.
36 Aylmer Bourke Lambert, *A Description of the Genus Pinus* (London, 1803), p. 74.
37 Euell Gibbons, *Stalking the Healthful Herbs* (New York, 1966), pp. 117–22.
38 John Davies, *Douglas of the Forests: The North American Journals of David Douglas* (Edinburgh, 1979), p. 64.

39 Helen Saberi, *Tea* (London, 2011), p. 16.
40 Mary Taylor Simeti, *Sicilian Food* (London, 1989), pp. 163–4.

6 Mythic Pine, Artist's Pine

1 Anon., *Cultus Arborum: A Descriptive Account of Phallic Tree Worship* (1890), p. 75.
2 Arthur Golding, trans., *Ovid's Metamorphoses* (Baltimore, MD, 2001), p. 56.
3 Nicholas T. Mirov and Jean Hasbrouck, *The Story of Pines* (Bloomington, IN, and London, 1976), p. 57.
4 Sir James Frazer, *The Golden Bough: A Study in Magic and Religion* (London, 1922), p. 387.
5 Ibid., pp. 347–8.
6 Ibid., p. 347.
7 Ibid., p. 352.
8 Ibid., p. 353.
9 Ibid., p. 354.
10 Walter Friedrich Otto, *Dionysos: Myth and Cult* (Bloomington, IN, 1995), p.134.
11 James W. Jackson, 'Villa of the Mysteries, Pompeii', www.art-and-archaeology.com, last accessed 23 October 2012.
12 Corrado Ricci and Ernesto Begni, *Vatican: Its History Its Treasures* (Whitefish, MT, 2003), pp. 45–6.
13 William M. Chiesa, *Non-Wood Forest Products from Conifers* (Rome, 1998), ch. 2, p. 1.
14 Anon., *Cultus Arborum*, pp. 93–4.
15 Ibid., p. 76.
16 Sharon Hudgins, *The Other Side of Russia* (College Station, TX, 2003), p. 134.
17 Ibid., p. 188.
18 Christopher McIntosh, *Gardens of the Gods: Myth, Magic and Meaning in Horticulture* (London, 2004), p. 49.
19 Patricia Bjaaland Welch, *Chinese Art: A Guide to Motifs and Visual Imagery* (North Clarendon, VT, 2008), p. 37.
20 Jake Hobson, *Niwaki: Pruning, Training and Shaping Trees the Japanese Way* (Portland, OR, 2007), p. 63.
21 Ibid.
22 Murasaki Shibuku, Royall Tyler, trans., *The Tale of Genji* (London, 2003), p. 432.
23 Hobson, *Niwaki*, p. 35.
24 Quoted by Chen Jun-yu and Zhang Shi Can, 'The World of Forestry', *Unasylva*, XXXI/126 (1979).
25 Hobson, *Niwaki*, p 63.
26 Ibid., p. 9.
27 Ibid., p. 35.
28 I am indebted to Ceri Oldham, kimono collector, for information about Japanese textiles.

29 Chiesa, *Non-Wood Forest Products from Conifers*, p. 4.
30 Leo Hickman, 'The Mammoth Camera', in *Guardian Review* (31 December 2011), pp. 14–15.
31 Ansel Adams, *The Portfolios of Ansel Adams with an Introduction by John Szarkowski* (Boston, MA, 1981). See, for instance, Portfolio III, plates 1, 5, 15; Portfolio IV, plate 2; Portfolio VI, plate 3.
32 Michael P. Cohen, *A Garden of Bristlecones* (Reno, NV, 1998), p. 212.
33 Ibid., p. 217.

7 The Sound of the Wind in the Branches

1 William Bray, ed., *The Diary of John Evelyn* (New York and London, 1901), vol. I, p. 228.
2 Mrs Ann Radcliffe, *The Mysteries of Udolpho* (New York, 1869), pp. 178–9.
3 Terry Gifford, *John Muir, His Life, Letters and Other Writings* (London and Seattle, WA, 1996), p. 321.
4 William Frederic Badè, ed., *Life and Letters of John Muir* (Boston, MA, 1924), vol. II, pp. 22–3.
5 Ibid., p. 309.
6 Robert Service, *Songs for My Supper* (New York, 1953).
7 Theodore Chickering Williams, trans., *Virgil: Georgics and Ecologues* (Cambridge, 1915), p. 155.
8 Leigh Hunt, 'The Nymphs Part II', in *Foliage: Poems Original and Translated* (London, 1818), p. XXII.
9 John Thompson, trans., 'Song of Wind Through the Pines', www.silkqin.com, last accessed 22 February 2013.
10 Gary Snyder, trans., 'Climbing Up the Cold Mountain', in *Poetry of HanShan*, www.chinapage.com, last accessed 22 February 2013.
11 Henry Wadsworth Longfellow, *Poetical Works* (New York, 1886), vol. II, p. 19.
12 Henry Wadsworth Longfellow, *The Song of Hiawatha* (London, 1855), p. 5.
13 Barry Cornwall, *The Poetical Works of Barry Cornwall* (London, 1822), vol. III, p. 121.
14 Ibid., p. 163.
15 Michael P. Cohen, *A Garden of Bristlecones* (Reno, NV, 1998), p. 213.
16 Perhaps best known as the music accompanying the whales in Walt Disney's *Fantasia 2000* (1999).
17 Albert J. von Frank and Thomas Wortham, eds, *The Collected Works of Ralph Waldo Emerson* (Cambridge, MA, 2011), vol. IX, p. 107.

Further Reading

Cohen, Michael P., *A Garden of Bristlecones* (Reno, NV, 1998)
Cole, James E., 'The Cone-bearing Trees of Yosemite', *Yosemite Nature Notes*, XVIII, 5 (1939)
Coppen, J.J.W., and G. A. Hone, *Gum Naval Stores: Turpentine and Rosin from Pine Resin* (Rome, 1995)
Davies, John, *Douglas of the Forests: The North American Journals of David Douglas* (Edinburgh, 1979)
Eckenwalder, James E., *Conifers of the World: The Complete Reference* (Portland, OR, 2009)
Evelyn, John, *Sylva, or a Discourse of Forest Trees and the Propogation of Timber: A Reprint of the 4th edn of 1716* (London, 1908)
Farjon, Aljos, *Pines: Drawings and Descriptions of the Genus Pinus,* 2nd edn (Leiden, 2005)
—, *A Natural History of Conifers* (Portland, OR, 2008)
Jepson, Willis Linn, *The Trees of California* (San Francisco, CA, 1909)
Lambert, Aylmer Bourke, *A Description of the Genus Pinus* (London, 1803)
Lanner, Ronald, *The Piñon Pine: A Natural and Cultural History* (Reno, NV, 1981)
—, *The Bristlecone Book: A Natural History of the World's Oldest Trees* (Missoula, MT, 2007)
Loudon, John Claudius, *An Encylopaedia of Trees and Shrubs, Being the Arboretum et Fructicetum Britannicum Abridged* (London, 1842)
McPhee, John, *The Pine Barrens* (New York, 1968)
Mieggs, Russell, *Trees and Timber in the Ancient Mediterranean World* (Oxford, 1982)
Mirov, Nicholas T., *The Genus Pinus* (New York, 1967)
Mirov, Nicholas T. and Jean Hasbrouck, *The Story of Pines* (Bloomington, IN, and London, 1976)
Outland III, Robert B., *Tapping the Pines: The Naval Stores Industry in the American South* (Baton Rouge, LA, 2004)
Perry, Jesse P., *The Pines of Mexico and Central America* (Portland, OR, 1991)
Richardson, David M., ed., *Ecology and Biogeography of Pinus* (Cambridge, 1998)
Tressider, Mary Curry, *Trees of Yosemite; A Popular Account* (Stanford, CT, 1932)

Associations and Websites

ARBORETUM DE VILLARDEBELLE
www.pinetum.org
Website that acts as a portal to pineta around the world, and hosts a conifer discussion group.

THE GYMNOSPERM DATABASE
www.conifers.org
Natural history, botany and taxonomy of conifers worldwide.

YOSEMITE ONLINE LIBRARY
www.yosemite.ca.us/library
Online books about Yosemite, including many about the trees of the American southwest.

PINON PENNY
www.pinenut.com
Website for a pine-nut harvesting business, including online ordering of pine nuts in season.

Acknowledgements

With grateful thanks to the Staff of York University Library and the British Library (St Pancras and Boston Spa). Ruth Grant drove me around Rothiemurchus, and Ceri Oldham, kimono collector, opened my eyes to pine patterns in Japanese textiles. Margaret and Will Grant helped with translations from the classics; Angela Davidson and Helen and Nasir Saberi brought pine nuts from far-flung places, and Chris Czajkowski allowed me to quote from her blog. Sheila Ward at the Forestry Commission and David Soulman at the UK Forest Products Association patiently answered my questions. Ivan Day and Gillian Riley helped with Italian recipes. Vienna Johnson and Agnes Winter provided support in the final stages of preparing the text. Erin Dodd, Caroline Hall, Linda Bolla, Valerie Jackson-Brown and John Wright provided assistance with illustrations and botanical detail. And thanks to Michael Leaman at Reaktion Books, who displayed exemplary patience, and to Derek Johnson, whose life was invaded by pine trees.

Photo Acknowledgements

The author and publishers wish to express their thanks to the below sources of illustrative material and/or permission to reproduce it. (Some information not placed in the captions for reasons of brevity is also given below.)

Photo afhunta/BigStockPhoto: p. 95; Art Gallery of Ontario, Toronto: p. 127; from J. J. Audubon, *Birds of America* (New York, 1840–44): p. 20; photos author: pp. 12, 16, 17, 29, 37, 50, 52, 82, 89, 108 (top), 125, 137, 144, 145; collection of the author: p. 185; photo John Baker: p. 86; photo basel101658/BigStockPhoto: pp. 34–5; Bibliothèque Nationale de France, Paris: p. 142; photo Derek Blair/Rex Features: p. 135; from Achilles Bocchius, *Achillis Bocchii Bonon. symbolicarum quaestionum de universo genere quas serio ludebat*... (Bologna, 1555): p. 55; from Hieronymus Bock, *Kreuter Büch, darin Underschied, Würckung und Namen der Kreüter so in Deutschen Landen wachsen*... (Strasburg, 1546): p. 59; British Museum, London (photos © Trustees of the British Museum): pp. 62, 91, 159, 161, 172, 192; photos © Trustees of the British Museum, London: pp. 49, 55, 56, 73, 88, 93, 150, 161, 173; photo ckchiu/BigStockPhoto: p. 6; Courtauld Institute of Art Gallery, London: p. 8; photo Chris Delanoue: p. 84; photo drknuth/BigStockPhoto: p. 164; from Rembert Doedens, *Stirpium historiae pemptades sex* (Antwerp, 1616): p. 64; from George Englemann, *Revision of the Genus 'Pinus' and Description of 'P. elliottii'* (St Louis, MO, 1880): p. 69; courtesy of the Erie Maritime Museum, Pennsylvania: p. 86; photo Ruth Grant: pp. 108 (foot), 113; photo habari1/2012 iStock International Inc: p. 14; illustration to Jan van der Heyden, *Beschryving der nieuwlijks uitgevonden en geoctrojeerde Slang-Brand-Spuiten, en Haare wyze van Brand-Blussen*... (Amsterdam, 1690): p. 93; photo igabriela/BigStockPhoto: pp. 154–5; photo Invicta Kent Media/Rex Features: p. 131; photo Kochergin/BigStockPhoto: p. 166; from Aylmer Bourke Lambert, *A Description of the Genus 'Pinus' illustrated with figures, directions relative to the cultivation, and remarks on the uses of the several species* (London, 1803–24): pp. 66, 70; photos Russell Lee: pp. 97, 132; photo jennifer leigh/BigStockPhoto: pp. 32–3; Library of Congress, Washington, DC: pp. 11, 97, 104–05, 118, 120, 123, 124, 132, 174, 175, 179, 181, 190–91; from Olaus Magnus, *Historia de Gentribus Septentrionalibus*... (Rome, 1555): pp. 63, 136; photos Janalice Merry: pp. 140, 146; images courtesy of the Missouri Botanical Garden Library: pp. 19, 69; illustration for an unidentified Latin edition of Sebastian Munster, *Cosmographia* (?Basel, 1544–52): p. 73; Museo Nationale Romano, Rome: p. 61; Museo del Prado, Madrid, Spain: p. 167; Museum für Kunst und Kulturgeschichte, Dortmund: p. 169; National Gallery of Art, Washington, DC: p. 116; National Gallery of Canada, Ottawa: p. 186; image courtesy of New Zealand Post Limited: p. 126; photo otme/2012 iStock International Inc.: p. 23; Palace Museum Collection, Taichung: p. 189; photo photosbyjim/2012 iStock International Inc.: p. 103; Frank A. Polkinghorn Jr: p. 115; from Pierre Pomet, *A Compleat History of Druggs* (London, 1737): pp. 58, 78; private collections: pp. 148, 170; photo S. M. Produkin-Gorskii: p. 118; photo Rigamondis/BigStockPhoto: p. 42; photo Roger-Viollet/Rex Features: p. 100; Sen-oku Hakuko Kan, Kyoto: p. 47; from the *Seventh Report of the Forest, Fish & Game Commission of the State of New York* (New York, 1902): p. 129; photo Jason Smith/2012 iStock International Inc.: pp. 40-41; Smithsonian American Art Museum, Washington, DC: p. 26, 44; photograph courtesy Spanierman Gallery, LLC, New York: p. 115; The State Russian Museum, St Petersburg: p. 114; State Tretyakov Gallery, Moscow: p. 46; from Sung Ying-hsing, *T'ien Kung K'ai Wu* (1637): p. 133; photos reproduced by kind permission of the Syndics of Cambridge University Library: pp. 58, 64, 66, 70, 78; Tokyo National Museum: pp. 176–7; from Joseph Pitton de Tournefort, *Corollarium Institutionum rei herbariae . . .*, vol. II (Paris, 1703): p. 19; U.S. Forest Service: p. 25; photo U.S. National Library of Medicine (History of Medicine Division), Bethesda, Maryland: p. 59; Vassar College Art Gallery, Poughkeepsie, New York: p. 83; The Warner Collection of Gulf States Paper Corporation, Tuscaloosa, Alabama: p. 45; from Maximilian zu Wied-Neuwied, *Maximilian Prince of Wied's Travels in the interior of North America during the years 1832–1834* (London, 1843–4): p. 112.

Index